LONG-TERM CONTROL OF
EXHAUSTIBLE RESOURCES

T0300497

FUNDAMENTALS OF PURE AND APPLIED ECONOMICS

EDITORS IN CHIEF

J. LESOURNE, Conservatoire National des Arts et Métiers, Paris, France
H. SONNENSCHEIN, University of Pennsylvania, Philadelphia, PA, USA

ADVISORY BOARD

ENVIRONMENTAL & NATURAL RESOURCE ECONOMICS
In 3 Volumes

I	Non-Renewable Resources Extraction Programs and Markets	
		Hartwick
II	Models of the Oil Market	*Crémer*
III	Long-Term Control of Exhaustible Resources	*Lasserre*

LONG-TERM CONTROL OF EXHAUSTIBLE RESOURCES

PIERRE LASSERRE

First published in 1991 by
Harwood Academic Publishers GmbH

Reprinted in 2001 by
Routledge
2 Park Square, Milton Park, Abingdon, Oxon OX14 4RN
711 Third Avenue, New York, NY 10017
Routledge is an imprint of the Taylor & Francis Group

First issued in paperback 2013

The publishers have made every effort to contact authors/copyright holders
of the works reprinted in *Harwood Fundamentals of Pure & Applied Economics*.
This has not been possible in every case, however, and we would welcome
correspondence from those individuals/companies we have been unable to
trace.

These reprints are taken from original copies of each book. in many cases
the condition of these originals is not perfect. the publisher has gone to
great lengths to ensure the quality of these reprints, but wishes to point
out that certain characteristics of the original copies will, of necessity, be
apparent in reprints thereof.

British Library Cataloguing in Publication Data
A CIP catalogue record for this book
is available from the British Library

ISBN13: 978-0-415-27462-3 (hbk)
ISBN13: 978-0-415-84933-3 (pbk)

Long-Term Control of Exhaustible Resources

by

Pierre Lasserre
Département des sciences économiques,
Université du Québec à Montréal

A volume in the Natural Resources and Environmental
Economics section
edited by
C. Henry
Ecole Polytechnique
Paris

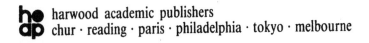 harwood academic publishers
chur · reading · paris · philadelphia · tokyo · melbourne

Harwood Academic Publishers

Post Office Box 90
Reading, Berkshire RG1 8JL
United Kingdom

3-14-9, Okubo
Shinjuku-ku, Tokyo 169
Japan

58, rue Lhomond
75005 Paris
France

Private Bag 8
Camberwell, Victoria 3124
Australia

5301 Tacony Street, Drawer 330
Philadelphia, Pennsylvania 19137
United States of America

Library of Congress Cataloging-in-Publication Data

Lasserre, Pierre.
    Long-term control of exhaustible resources / Pierre Lasserre.
        p. cm. — (Fundamentals of pure and applied economics, ISSN 0191-1708; v.
    49. Natural resources and environmental economics section)
    Includes bibliographical references and index.
    ISBN 3-7186-5134-3
    1. Natural resources. I. Title. II. Series: Fundamentals of
    pure and applied economics; v. 49. III. Series: Fundamentals of
    pure and applied economics. Natural resources and environmental
    economics section.
    HC59.L348   1991
    333.7—dc20

91-763
CIP

Contents

Introduction to the Series vii

INTRODUCTION 1

1. MAJOR THEORETICAL RESULTS 4
 1.1 Hotelling rule and the views of Ricardo. 4
 1.2 The individual mine. 9
 1.3 Economic reserves and exhaustion. 10
 1.4 Aggregation. 11
 1.5 Exploration. 12
 1.6 Sectoral extraction and the behaviour of price. 13
 1.7 Multiple deposits, capital, and other complications. 14
 1.8 Welfare, competition, and stability. 16
 1.9 Other imperfections. 21
 1.10 Growth and survival. 22
 1.11 Monopoly. 27
 1.12 Duopoly and oligopoly. 30

2. EMPIRICAL TESTS AND PRICE STUDIES 37
 2.1 Reminder. 37
 2.2 Evidence on scarcity rents. 39
 2.3 Evidence on the behaviour of rents and prices over time. 40

3. JOINT PRODUCTS AND THE ENVIRONMENT 43
 3.1 Introduction. 43
 3.2 Joint production from composite reserves. 44
 3.3. Optimum pollution stocks and clean-up. 49
 3.4 Transnational pollution in general equilibrium. 54

4. TRADE AND MACROECONOMIC ISSUES 56
 4.1 Resource models with trade: survival revisited. 56
 4.2 Trade models with natural resources: the basic trade theorems. 59
 4.3 The Dutch Disease and the Macroeconomy. 69
 4.4 Other issues. 79

5. TAXATION   82
   5.1   Introduction.   82
   5.2   Resource taxation in a simple Hotelling world.   83
   5.3   Resource taxation in a simple Ricardian world.   90
   5.4   The corporate income tax.   99
   5.5   Exploration.   104
   5.6   Optimal taxation and tax incidence in general
       equilibrium.   109

Bibliography   111
Index   120

Introduction to the Series

Drawing on a personal network, an economist can still relatively easily stay well informed in the narrow field in which he works, but to keep up with the development of economics as a whole is a much more formidable challenge. Economists are confronted with difficulties associated with the rapid development of their discipline. There is a risk of 'balkanization' in economics, which may not be favorable to its development.

Fundamentals of Pure and Applied Economics has been created to meet this problem. The discipline of economics has been subdivided into sections (listed at the back of this volume). These sections comprise short books, each surveying the state of the art in a given area.

Each book starts with the basic elements and goes as far as the most advanced results. Each should be useful to professors needing material for lectures, to graduate students looking for a global view of a particular subject, to professional economists wishing to keep up with the development of their science, and to researchers seeking convenient information on questions that incidentally appear in their work.

Each book is thus a presentation of the state of the art in a particular field rather than a step-by-step analysis of the development of the literature. Each is a high-level presentation but accessible to anyone with a solid background in economics, whether engaged in business, government, international organizations, teaching, or research in related fields.

Three aspects of *Fundamentals of Pure and Applied Economics* should be emphasized:

— First, the project covers the whole field of economics, not only theoretical or mathematical economics.
— Second, the project is open-ended and the number of books is not predetermined. If new and interesting areas appear, they will generate additional books.

—Last, all the books making up each section will later be grouped to constitute one or several volumes of an Encyclopedia of Economics.

The editors of the sections are outstanding economists who have selected as authors for the series some of the finest specialists in the world.

J. Lesourne   *H. Sonnenschein*

Long-Term Control of Exhaustible Resources

PIERRE LASSERRE

Département des sciences économiques,
Université du Québec à Montréal

INTRODUCTION

Natural resources, especially exhaustible and non-renewable ones, have understandably always been a matter of concern to economists, politicians and even philosophers. Over time, this attention has taken various forms and experienced spurs of intense controversy alternating with periods of relative calm.

Resources have been important dimensions of economic development and the shaping of history. Major population movements have often been explained by economic considerations, in particular the availability of certain resources. Key steps in the development of modern economies have usually taken place in conjunction with the exploitation of some crucial natural resource while the realization of such dependency prompted the intellectual developments which shaped the discipline now known as natural-resource economics.

While early economists such as the mercantilists were keenly aware of the importance of adequate supplies, natural resources, in fact basically the issue of food supply, were first given a truly specific treatment with the work of Malthus, Ricardo, and Mill. Non-renewable resources only became the focus of much attention when Jevons raised The Coal Question (1865). If the British industrial revolution was made possible by the availability of coal as a source of energy, what was to be expected when coal reserves were to run out? Similar issues were to be raised recurrently during the following decades, the most recent version dating back to the recent oil crisis.

This monograph is concerned with the modern theory of non-renewable resource exploitation and its empirical implications. This is

1

a very broad and rich area; it is impossible to do it justice within sensible space constraints. The necessary compromise between completeness and depth of coverage is reflected in the organization of the monograph. Two basic sections, one theoretical, one empirical, provide a broad coverage of most important issues. The approach is analytical and formalized, but technical details are left out whenever they do not contribute to the understanding of a question. Then there are three additional sections, which cover specific areas in more detail. The choice of these areas was motivated by various considerations. In the case of Section 3, on joint products and the environment, it is the desire to put more emphasis on a subject and on methodologies that have not received enough attention in the literature. In the case of Section 4, on trade and the macroeconomy, I want to underline both the extensive work done to deal with natural-resource considerations, and the limits of current knowledge and approaches in that respect. Finally, in the case of Section 5, on resource taxation, the idea is to provide a unified and organized treatment of an area which is both very rich and difficult to approach without guidance.

Exhaustibility was one dimension of Jevons' concern. This dimension constitutes a major facet of modern resource economics, one often associated with the name of Hotelling. However growing scarcity is also manifest in the substitution of lower quality, or more costly, supply sources for the disappearing ones. This notion of Ricardian scarcity is also fundamental in the discipline. Section 1 starts by presenting the Hotelling and the Ricardian view and goes on contrasting their implications for the individual mine. The notion of economic reserves, the concept and desirability of exhaustion are then examined, and various complications are introduced: aggregation, exploration, as well as sectoral extraction and price. This may give the impression that exhaustible resource economics is a very specific area, one very remote from standard microeconomics. Quite the contrary, it is solidly rooted into the standard apparatus, as indicated by a discussion of welfare, competition, stability, and the issue of growth and survival. However, while standard economic theorems usually survive their transposition to a resource context, exhaustibility often affects the results in surprising ways. At first competition looks like monopoly; then it is found that monopoly does not differ from competition in the same way as in the standard analysis. In all cases, the analysis has to be dynamic and this is perhaps the main specificity of resource economics.

This emphasis on dynamic properties carries through to the empirical implications and tests of the theory, presented in Section 2. They fall into two broad categories, each corresponding to specific questions. First, is resource scarcity an issue? How can scarcity be measured? Are scarcity rents observable and what is their importance? Second, if scarcity is indeed an issue, do the dynamics of prices and rents conform to the predictions of the theory? The answer to this question should be easy to check. It is not, because it turns out that the predictions of the theory are clear-cut only under highly restrictive assumptions. As a result, many tests can be interpreted as tests of these assumptions rather than the fundamentals of the theory; the evidence is very ambiguous.

The three sections on special topics are very different from each other. Section 3, on joint products, starts with an analysis of joint production from composite reserves. This is not only empirically relevant: copper is most frequently associated with gold, and oil with gas. But joint production is also a natural way to approach environmental issues: smoke is produced as a by-product of many activities. Furthermore, the economics of non-renewable resources apply well to environmental issues. As argued later in the section, the environment can be viewed as finite, and its management as the mirror image of a mining problem: that of filling up a mine of finite capacity instead of removing material from it. While this brings up the dynamic aspects of external effects, the standard static approach may also be enlightening, as illustrated by the analysis of transnational pollution which closes the section.

Section 4, on trade and macroeconomic issues, starts with a clarification on the implications of trade for survival. Then it surveys the extensions of trade theory to resource contexts; despite considerable efforts trade theory remains unable to handle the most interesting issues raised by exhaustible resources. The literature on the Dutch desease, the major incursion of macroeconomics into natural resources, is also surveyed in the section. Here one finds that there was no attempt to incorporate the dynamics of resource constraints into the analysis, which remains basically static. The natural resource is treated as any other sector experiencing a real shock and motivates the comparative static analysis of that shock.

Section 5 deals with resource taxation. Taxation has been recognized as a very important aspect of resource exploitation, in part because the tax function doubles with that of collecting resource rents. An abundant literature studies the effects of numerous taxes; unlike the previous topic, it emanates from the resource literature directly. However, because it is technically involving and lacks uniformity in both methodology and areas of relevance, it is of difficult access to the non-specialist. While not devoid of technical difficulties, the treatment presented in Section 5 is progressive and uniform, starting with the effect of a royalty on a simple Hotelling mine and finishing, before turning to general equilibrium considerations, with a firm which holds heterogeneous reserves, is involved in exploration activities, and uses capital. This should leave the reader with a good understanding of both results and methodology.

Acknowledgement The author gratefully acknowledges financial support by the Université de Montréal, the Fonds FCAR pour l'aide et le soutien à la recherche, and the Social Sciences and Humanities Research Council of Canada. Part of the work was done while the author was on sabbatical leave at the Sloan School, which provided a stimulating environment as well as material support. Thanks are extended to Ernie Berndt, Robert Cairns, Gérard Gaudet, Tracy Lewis, John Livernois, Michel Moreaux, Robert Pindyck, Steve Salant, Anthony Scott, Margaret Slade, Ngo Van Long, who helped shape my understanding of resource economics over the years. I owe a special debt to Robert Cairns who made highly valuable comments on this monograph.

1. MAJOR THEORETICAL RESULTS

1.1. Hotelling rule and the views of Ricardo

Although Hotelling and Ricardo are probably the most widely quoted economists when it comes to resource economics, their perceptions of important realities are widely opposed. To Hotelling (1931), exhaustibility and non-renewability are the important characteristics to emphasize. In the Ricardian view, the resource sector is heterogeneous; supply sources differ in quality and their mix in equilibrium adjusts to demand. Exhaustibility is not really an issue, although depletion may be manifest in a drop in the quality of supply sources. It should also be recognized that Hotelling and Ricardo share with other authors the paternity of the ideas attributed to them. In particular, Gray (1914) studied the case of the individual competitive nine years before Hotelling (Crabbé, 1983).

Hotelling

In the world of Hotelling, the economy, just like the extractive firms which compose its resource sector, is endowed at time t with a finite resource stock $S(t)$ whose consumption provides utility directly or, equivalently, which can be used to produce some consumption good. At what rate should this stock be depleted and when should exhaustion occur? Should the familiar rules governing supply decisions, such as the equality of price and marginal cost, be applied? Hotelling's model produced strong results which were in sharp contrast with conventional economic wisdom. They also emphasized time and dynamic aspects. In particular, it is socially desirable that price be set above marginal cost[1] by an amount identified as the scarcity rent. This rent represents the value conferred to the resource, over and above extraction and processing costs, by the fact that it will be exhausted some day. Its reflection in the price is desirable because it slows down extraction, thus postponing exhaustion.

The finite resource stock available to society is homogeneous, which means not only that it is of uniform quality, but that it is concentrated in a single location and that any unit of it is accessible at the same constant cost. Once these assumptions are made, there is no loss in further assuming extraction costs to be zero, which produces the most extreme version of the so-called 'Hotelling rule' to be explained below.

Although Hotelling studied both the behaviour of individual extractive firms and the point of view of society as a whole, I shall consider the latter case here, and present a most simple version of the model. Society attempts to maximize a rising and concave social welfare function defined on aggregate consumption c, over a possibly infinite period $[0, T]$:

$$\int_O^T e^{-rt} U(c(t)) \, dt.$$

---

[1] Hotelling actually assumes marginal cost to be zero.

r is the constant discount rate. U is defined as the consumer surplus arising from consumption in any period; consequently, as is well known, its first derivative U' is equal to the price $p(t)$. The assumption that social welfare is additively separable over time is analytically convenient but not crucial to the results. As a second convenient simplification, it is assumed that consumption is drawn from the resource stock directly and at no cost

$$c(t) = - dS/dt \text{ with } S(0) = S_o,$$

the given initial reserve stock. The current value Hamiltonian associated with this constrained maximization is

$$h(c) = U(c) - \mu c$$

where μ is the costate variable associated with S, expressed in current value.[2] Commonly referred to as the *Hotelling rent*, or *scarcity rent*, it measures the opportunity cost of foregoing future consumption by extracting one marginal unit of the reserve stock at the current date. As a necessary condition we have[3]

$$U'(c) = \mu \qquad \text{or} \qquad p = \mu.$$

Although the resource is free in the sense that it can be extracted at zero cost, it is not freely available in all future time periods but is scarce. As a result, μ is strictly positive for finite values of S, so that consumption does not occur at an infinite rate. Price is optimally set strictly above marginal cost (zero). A gap between price and extraction cost need not be interpreted as a sign that market power is being exercised. It is socially optimal, from a global point of view, for Saudi Arabia to sell oil for more than its extraction cost. By how much should price exceed marginal cost? This is another issue to be discussed further below.

A second necessary condition is

$$d\mu/dt = r\mu(t)$$

or, since $p = \mu$

$$(dp/dt)/p = r. \qquad (1.1)$$

---

[2] The conventionally defined Hamiltonian is $H(c,t) = e^{-rt}U(c) - M c$, being the costate variable associated with S; thus $\mu = M e^{rt}$.

[3] Time arguments are omitted where no ambiguity arises.

Price should rise at the rate of discount. This result is known as *Hotelling rule* and has raised much interest and controversy. As we shall see, it usually fails to be verified empirically. On the other hand, it has such an obvious interpretation and stems so directly from basic capital theory that economists have attempted to improve upon the model rather than discard the basic methodology which underlies Hotelling's approach.

The interpretation of Hotelling rule is indeed straightforward. In the model mineral reserves represent an asset which is costlessly stored underground. If they are to be held willfully, their return must be comparable to the return on other assets. Being otherwise unproductive, reserves must produce capital gains at the rate of interest.

Hotelling's model also clarifies the issue of exhaustion. Suppose exhaustion is to occur at a finite date T. Then the condition $U' = \mu = p$ must hold at T in particular.

$$U'(c(T)) = p(T)$$

Suppose $c(T) = c^+$ was strictly positive. Then, by splitting c^+ and consuming, say $c^+/2$ at T and $c^+/2$ the instant after, at $T + \epsilon$, one could achieve a higher level of total discounted utility. This is so because $U'(c^+/2) > U'(c^+)$ for any downward-sloping demand curve. Consequently, in the socially optimum program, consumption must decrease toward zero when exhaustion is near; simultaneously, price must rise toward $p(T) = U'(0)$. If $U'(0) = \infty$, with price rising at the discount rate by (1.1), this cannot occur in a finite period; but if $U'(0)$ is finite, exhaustion will occur at a finite date T. In other words, if a resource is so important that its demand does not vanish when its price looms very high, society will spread its consumption very thinly over time so as not to exhaust it. It is optimal to exhaust oil reserves some day (as we have already lived without oil); but if no substitute form of energy was available, it might well be desirable to avoid such an outcome. As we shall see, this idea that some resources may be more crucial than others, and the issue of survival, were addressed in more detail by several authors. Presently however let us contrast Hotelling's view with that of Ricardo.

Ricardo

Ricardo (1817) was not interested in exhaustible resources explicitly, although he was concerned with the finiteness of good agricultural land. In his view, food supply adjusts to growing population and wealth through the cultivation of new land areas. The best quality lands, in terms of fertility, ease of cultivation, and market proximity, are put into production first. As demand increases, lower quality lands are cultivated, so that, at any one time, lands of varying fertility and characteristics are observed to contribute to food supply. Since the best lands produce the same food as the worst ones, but at a lower cost, and since food commands a uniform price, price exceeds marginal cost on all but the least productive units. The marginal land is that unit which barely covers its costs at the going price. All other units earn *Ricardian rents* on the excess of price over cost.

Exhaustibility is clearly not an issue here, as land, in a first approximation, is renewable in the sense that it remains available for future production. Ricardo's conceptualization does translate to exhaustible non-renewable resources though. Minerals are distributed into the earth crust non-uniformly. A deposit is the combined occurrence of a high enough grade, in sufficient volume, at a depth and location which permit extraction at reasonable costs. These conditions leave room for a tremendous variety among the mineral occurrences which qualify as deposits at any one time. For some deposits, price barely meets extraction costs while some others, as the best Ricardian agricultural lands, command a substantial rent.

Thus it is clear that some resource rents are Ricardian rents, not scarcity rents in the sense of Hotelling. On the other hand, mineral deposits do get exhausted, unlike land, and this implies that any deposit may command a scarcity rent. Consequently, prices and rents must satisfy some dynamic rule, in the spirit of Hotelling rule, which reflects the capital theoretic nature of extraction decisions. The real world probably stands somewhere between the Hotelling and the Ricardian representations.

In the next sub sections, I present some of the important theoretical results which have been obtained on various issues, by studying models which will be recognized to have a Ricardian bent or a Hotelling flavour alternatively or simultaneously. The choice of issues has been dictated by empirical relevance and also the traditional preoccupations of the economic profession. Thus the social optimality of perfect competition and the validity of the first and second theorems of welfare economics, have been investigated in a world involving non-renewable resources. Competitive and monopolistic behaviour have been contrasted, both between each other and from the point of view of standard monopoly theory. The point of view of growth theorists has also been adapted to a world with non-renewable resources, with the study of such issues as survival, growth in *per capita* consumption, and the importance of technological change.

1.2. The individual mine

The microeconomic problem of the individual mine was formally investigated by Gray (1914) much before Hotelling published his famous paper, which can be viewed as an aggregate, sectoral, treatment of the extraction problem. Gray had actually anticipated many of the refinements introduced later in order to provide a treatment which was more in conformity with the technological and geological reality and the textbook treatment of the conventional firm. In particular, marginal cost was made a rising function of the extraction flow $R(t)$ and the resource stock was allowed to be heterogeneous.

This heterogeneity has several dimensions: mineral deposits and oil fields differ in grade, viscosity, depth, volume, shape, location, site, the types of minerals found above and inside them, etc ... While it may be physical or economic, heterogeneity implies that extraction costs vary over the extraction program for reasons other than extraction rates. One fruitful way to model this property has been to let extraction costs depend, besides output rate, on the remaining reserve stock. In its simple version the idea is that extraction becomes more costly as the deposit becomes depleted; in a more sophisticated rationalization, it is argued that the order of extraction for the various parts of a deposit is selected optimally, and optimality requires that low-cost resources be extracted first. The validity of this postulate, which is further discussed in section 1.6, should be demonstrated as part of the solution.

This approach implies a cost function of the form $C(R, S)$, with $C_s \leq 0$. Such a function was introduced by Levhari and Liviatan (1977). Thus the competitive firm maximizes the present value of revenues minus costs with cumulative extraction required to remain lower than initial reserves

$$Max \int_0^T e^{-rt} [p(t) R(t) - C(R(t), S(t))] dt$$

subject to

$$- dS/dt = R(t) \text{ with } S(0) = S_o \text{ and } S(t) \geq 0 \text{ at all dates.}$$
$$(1.2)$$

Here, $p(t)$ is treated as exogenous to the firm, and T must be interpreted as the endogenous date at which the firm shuts down its operations, whether or not reserves have been exhausted. In order to rule out such complications as temporary interruptions in production, it is assumed that $p(t)$ always is high enough to cover costs and does not rise faster than at the discount rate. A sufficient condition for existence of a solution is joint convexity of $C(\cdot)$ in R and S; however, a solution also exists if average cost is convex in R and has a minimum at $\underline{R(S)}$ (Lewis, 1979). Under these assumptions, the solution must satisfy the Maximum principle, so that price equals marginal cost plus rent, a sum often called full marginal cost

$$p = \partial C(R, S)/\partial R + \mu. \qquad (1.3)$$

The rule according to which the rent rises at the interest rate is now mitigated by a correction for changes in reserve quality, as measured by the correlation between S and C

$$d\mu/dt = r\mu + \partial C(R, S)/\partial S, \text{ or}$$

$$\mu(t) = \mu(T) e^{-r(T-t)} - \int_{t}^{T} e^{-r(s-t)} (\partial C(R, S)/\partial S) ds \qquad (1.4)$$

The rent at t is the discounted rent at T plus the cumulated present value of all future effects on extraction cost of extracting the marginal unit at t. Because it reflects quality differences in the resource, the second term is interpreted as the Ricardian component of the rent while the first one is interpreted as the scarcity component (or Hotelling rent)[4] and may vanish under some configurations.

1.3. Economic reserves and exhaustion

The desirability of exhausting a deposit completely is closely linked to the presence of a Hotelling rent. At T, by the transversality condition on S, either $\mu > 0$ and $S = 0$ (complete exhaustion), or $\mu = 0$

---

[4] This interpretation is more meaningful when the model is used as a sectoral model, as in Levhari and Liviatan (1977).

and $S \geq 0$ (some resource is left in the ground). In both cases, the Hamiltonian must also vanish which, combined with (1.3), implies that extraction is carried out at a terminal rate which minimizes average cost. The Hotelling component of the rent is positive and exhaustion is optimal if price exceeds minimum average cost when reserves are down to zero; in fact, at any time, the Hotelling component of the rent is the present value of that gap. This is null if, as in the alternative possibility, there exists a positive level of reserves $S(T)$ below which minimum average cost exceeds price. This criterion may be used to define economic reserves; as one expects, non-economic reserves are left in the ground at T, and the definition is conditional on price at T^5.

1.4. Aggregation

These results are valid in the aggregate when the Hicksian aggregation criterion applies. But according to that criterion, in order to be considered identical, firms must have identical deposits. When this is true, rents are identical in all firms i, so that, by (1.3), marginal costs are equalized. In general, however, $\mu^i \neq \mu^j$ and marginal costs differ across firms.

Aggregation problems are now known to be acute in the presence of non-renewable resources. Blackorby and Schworm (1984) have shown that both the model with costs that rise as aggregate reserves diminish, and the Hotelling model in which aggregate revenues depend only on aggregate extraction rate, are inconsistent with the micro-economic reality which they aim to reflect. However, the modelling approach just described has routinely been applied at the sectoral level and has shaped what is now conventional wisdom on resource extraction in the aggregate. While some authors have explicitly attempted to treat a resource industry as a set of individual mines or deposits (see Section 1.6), several major sectoral results are based on the assumption of a single reserve stock and are vulnerable to the same kind of critiques which had occupied capital theorists *ad nauseam* for two decades when some of them turned to resource economics in the early

---

^{5} If price rises after T, the competitive mine will stay in production in such a way as to maintain economic reserves at zero; in other words, it will ensure that, for $t \geq T$, $C[\underline{R}(S), S]/R(S) = p$.

seventies. For example Schultze (1974), who first explicitely modelled the entry and exit of mines characterized by U-shaped cost curves, and worked out the resulting sector price equilibrium trajectory, assumed all firms to extract from a common reserve stock rented out to them by some central planner.

1.5. Exploration[6]

In the extraction model described so far, it is assumed that ultimate reserves are limited to the known existing stock. Of course this is an oversimplification, which was criticized by many, including Benzoni (1988). Discoveries keep replenishing reserves; it is not uncommon for an extractive sector to experience a rise in reserves despite extraction.

In order to give the simple extraction model some realism, one may treat reserves as inclusive of future discoveries, which are uncertain. This has given rise to a literature on 'how to eat a cake or uncertain size' (Kemp, 1976; Loury, 1978; Robson, 1979).

As a more ambitious alternative, the exploration process may be introduced explicitely. Exploration may perform a combination of three basic functions. The first, perhaps the least crucial one, is to help reduce current and future extraction costs. In the Ricardian model presented above, higher reserves mean lower costs, which would be one explanation why firms do explore and hold reserves (Pindyck, 1978b, 1980). This view has been challenged on the ground that newly discovered reserves are often more costly to extract (Cairns, 1991).

The second, and most obvious, function of exploration is to generate discoveries, so that reserves are sufficient to permit extraction at a rate compatible with demand. As it is desirable to postpone exploration expenditures for as long as possible, reserves are allowed to go down to the lowest level compatible with an acceptable risk of supply disruption before they are replenished (Arrow and Chang, 1982). The rent rises as reserves diminish, and falls upon new discoveries. Ultimate scarcity depends on the availability of exploration prospects, and Hotelling rule is modified accordingly. If exploration prospects are infinite, as in Deshmuck and Pliska (1980), long-run resource prices are not expected to rise on average. If exploration prospects are limited, an attenuated version of Hotelling rule governs resource prices

---

[6] A simple model of exploration is also presented in the chapter on taxation.

(Lasserre, 1984). They rise on average, but at a rate lower than the interest rate.

However, as a third function, exploration also provides new information about undiscovered reserves; by updating estimates of remaining reserves in the light of exploration results, the planner may improve the use of the cake of unknown size over time (Gilbert, 1979). The first and the second functions have been combined into a single model by Quyen (1989). Bayesian up-dating enriches the model substantially. At any date of exploration, the higher the amount of resource discovered, the lower the resource price after discovery, which reflects the normal reaction to lucky outcomes, but also the higher the threshold reserve level at which exploration will resume, which reflects more optimism about future prospects. A major difference with the results of Lasserre is that the realized time path of the resource price may then exhibit a diminishing trend as a result of such revisions.

1.6. Sectoral extraction and the behaviour of price

Treating (1.3) and (1.4) as sectoral relationships and letting $p(t) = P(R(t))$ so that aggregate demand determines the equilibrium price for any output level, one has, by differentiating (1.3) and substituting for μ and $d\mu/dt$

$$dp/dt = (\partial P/\partial R)dR/dt =$$
$$(\partial^2 C/\partial R^2)dR/dt + (\partial^2 C/\partial R\partial S)dS/dt$$
$$+ r(p - \partial C/\partial R) + \partial C/\partial S \qquad (1.5)$$

or

$$(\partial P/\partial R - \partial^2 C/\partial R^2)dR/dt = (\partial^2 C/\partial R\partial S)dS/dt$$
$$+ r(p - \partial C/\partial R) + \partial C/\partial S. \qquad (1.6)$$

Since $\partial P/\partial R < 0$, it is clear from (1.5) that a sufficient condition for a rising price is for extraction to decrease over time. (1.6) clarifies under which circumstances this turns out to be the case. Assuming non-diminishing marginal costs ($\partial^2 C/\partial R^2 \geq 0$), the coefficient of dR/dt is negative; consequently dR/dt is negative if the right-hand side of (1.6) is positive. Although marginal extraction costs are probably non-increasing in reserves ($\partial^2 C/\partial R\partial S \leq 0$) so that the first term on the right-hand side is non-negative, the term $\partial C/\partial S$, which accounts for

the heterogeneity of reserves may dominate the first two terms, implying a decreasing price trajectory in equilibrium.

Thus the presence of Ricardian characteristics mitigates Hotelling's
prediction of a net price rising at the rate of interest. If the Hotelling
component of the rent (second term on the right-hand side of (1.6))
is small and reserves are very heterogeneous (strong third term on the
right-hand-side of (1.6)), the price may even diminish. However, as
Slade (1982b) pointed out, if the Hotelling component is present at all,
since it rises exponentially, it is likely to start dominating the other
terms over a long enough period.

1.7. Multiple deposits, capital, and other complications

At the microeconomic level, the Ricardian view implies that some
deposits may be in production while some may not. But while, in the
conventional agricultural interpretation, only demand conditions
determine whether land will be in production or out of production,
supply conditions keep changing in extractive sectors. In fact, unlike
agricultural land, deposits become exhausted and supply sources must
be replaced.

Herfindahl (1967) argued that the resource should be depleted in
strict sequence, beginning with the lowest cost deposit and progressing
to the highest cost. This view is in contrast with empirical evidence;
in a partial equilibrium framework, it relies on the assumption of
constant marginal cost; in a general equilibrium framework, other
issues come under consideration. Hartwick (1978) was the first to
attempt a general treatment. Several authors have also contributed to
clarify the analysis. Generalizing the earlier work of Solow and Wan
(1977), Lewis (1982) showed that sequential order is optimal if the
resource can be converted into consumable or storable capital, while
Kemp and Long (1980c) discussed the meaning of the constant
marginal cost assumption underlying the result, in a general equilibrium growth context. Salant, Eswaran, and Lewis (1983) studied the
length of the optimal extraction path, showing in particular that
infinite time might be optimal even if the price at which demand chokes
off is finite.

There is intuitive appeal to a behaviour consisting in postponing
expenditures for as long as possible; but since full marginal cost not
only varies with output, but also includes rent, which is itself affected

by deposit size, the notion of least cost deposit must be treated cautiously. In most reasonably general cost configurations, social optimality requires simultaneous exploitation of several deposits (Cairns and Lasserre, 1986; Hung, 1986). Furthermore, Slade (1988) argues that none of the non-stochastic, theoretically-derived, order-of-extraction rules is consistent with empirical regularities in mineral-industry extraction profiles. Those regularities—a secular decline in both present-value price and average grade of ores mined, combined with a negative correlation between grade and price over the business cycle—are compatible with the predictions of Slade's model where prices are driven by a martingale process and firms hold rational expectations.

It is not clear that this literature provides much more information on theoretical resource price paths than the aggregate model of Levhari and Liviatan presented above; however, most models (see, e.g. Hanson, 1980; Hung, 1986) predict price to rise, at a rate lower than the discount rate, and conclude that situations of declining resource prices are either impossible or exceptional. One such exception occurs when firms have to build up capacity in order to produce (Puu, 1977; Campbell, 1980; Kemp and Long, 1984a; Gaudet, 1983; Lasserre, 1985a); in such circumstances, Cairns and Lasserre (1986) show that young resource sectors may be characterized by decreasing prices, although prices sooner or later will be on a rising trend. They also show that rigid capacities may cause short-run swings around a rising long-run trend, a widely empirically observed phenomenon which was studied by Slade (1982a; 1988). Another benefit of keeping track of individual firms within a sector has been to point to the variety of individual behaviours and circumstances which may coexist in a resource sector. Firms may be out of production because they have exhausted their reserves or because they delay production; when they produce, their output may be increasing or decreasing irrespective of what happens to sectoral output[7]. Finally, oligopoly situations may result in simultaneous extraction even when social optimality requires a strict sequence. Although they do not address that issue explicitly, several of the oligopoly models presented in Section 1.12 illustrate this phenomenon.

---

[7] In fact this Ricardian analysis of sectoral production has led some authors to modify the conventional treatment of the individual mine to take account of quality variations within individual deposits (Krautkraemer, 1989; Cairns, 1986).

Closely related to the Ricardian view is the treatment of resource substitutes. Nordhaus (1973) first coined the term of 'backstop' technology to refer to a technology which can be introduced as a substitute for a less expensive one. The existence of that technology puts a ceiling on the price which can be asked for the less expensive source. For example, in Figure 1.3, if p is the price of oil, p^{max} may be the price of nuclear energy. The backstop technology is usually considered to be reproducible; however, it can be an alternative exhaustible resource, as when coal is considered an alternative to oil. In fact, Nordhaus provided a world model of energy supply with an estimation of the order, dates, and prices of introduction of alternative supply sources into the third millennia. While Nordhaus' model was more empirical and heuristic than analytical, his basic idea stimulated much theoretical work. In all those papers, a single natural resource is available in finite amount and must eventually be replaced by a reproducible alternative. In the early versions (e.g. Hoel, 1978), the reserve stock is known, the cost of the alternative source is known and constant, and competitive or monopolistic behaviours are envisaged. In more recent contributions, the authors have relaxed one or several of those assumptions. Alternative market structures and strategic behaviours were considered by Salant (1979), Stiglitz and Dasgupta (1982), Hoel (1983), and Hung et al. (1984); the size of reserves, the cost of producing the substitute, or the date of the discovery which is to make it available, were treated as uncertain or endogenous (Kemp and Long, 1982a). Reinganum and Stockey (1985) treated the research for the substitute as a racing game while Swierzbinski and Mendelsohn (1989) focused on the implications of the fact that firms measure such relevant data as the cost of a substitute with endogeneous precision.

1.8. Welfare, competition, and stability

From a welfare point of view, exploiting a non-renewable resource is a problem of allocating a finite stock of a commodity between competing uses at different dates. As is well known, the competitive equilibrium in such an intertemporal set-up yields an efficient allocation provided, among other conditions, a complete set of forward markets exists. If agents can trade the resource now for all future dates, they have the necessary information to compute the value of using one unit of the resource at one particular date relative to some other date. But this is precisely the information required to compute μ in a formula such as (1.3). Although the presence of a wedge between price and marginal cost does not fit the usual description of an efficient equilibrium, (1.3) is clearly a necessary condition for efficiency since it has been obtained as a first-order condition for competitive profit maximization. In fact the apparent contradiction is easily reconciled when the rent is recognized to be part of the marginal cost, as it measures the cost, in terms of lost future revenues, of using one marginal unit of reserves.

While the detailed implications of adapting the intertemporal Walrasian framework to a world involving non-renewable resources have been investigated and described well (see, e.g. Dasgupta and Heal, 1979, chapters 4 and 8; de La Grandville, 1980), the real question is whether 'the absence of futures and risk markets is any more serious for the intertemporal allocation of natural resources than it is, say, for the allocation of investment' (Stiglitz, 1974b). One major difference which comes to one's mind is the fact that, while errors in the capital accumulation programme can be corrected at some cost, extraction decisions are irreversible and may have very costly consequences if mistakes are discovered too late. The issues of long-run stability and short-run adjustment become crucial from that point of view.

In the absence of a complete set of forward markets, firms will make extraction decisions according to a modified version of (1.5) where the price p and the inverse demand function P must be interpreted as expectations[8]. Similarly, μ must be interpreted as the expected value of the rent. The issue of stability can be illustrated as follows. Consider the dynamic system [(1.2); (1.3); (1.4)]; as discussed earlier, this system may alternatively imply ultimate exhaustion (presence of a positive Hotelling's component in the rent) or a strictly positive stock of reserves may be left in the ground at T (the strictly Ricardian case); let us focus on the second possibility. A momentary equilibrium is a situation where expectations are fulfilled; assume that such is the case in (1.2)–(1.4) so that μ represents both the actual and the expected rent which will be treated as a price. It is easily shown that the dynamic system has a steady-state, long-run, equilibrium ($S^* = S(T)$; $\mu^* = 0$) where extraction has stopped. This steady state reflects the transversality

---

[8] This assumes that the modified, stochastic, problem admits (1.5) as a certainty equivalent form. Although this is not the case in general, more generality in this context would only obscure the treatment of the problem.

conditions discussed earlier (Section 1.3). Indeed S^* is the reserve level below which the minimum unit extraction cost exceeds the price; it is optimal to leave the remaining reserves in the ground forever and, accordingly, to assign a value of $\mu^* = 0$ to the marginal reserve unit. Let us characterize the behaviour of the dynamic system in a neighbourhood of the steady state equilibrium, that is to say in situations which may be considered delicate, as the resource is about to become too costly to extract, hence unavailable.

In the tradition initiated by Hahn (1966), it has been argued by Stiglitz (1974a) and Dasgupta and Heal (1974, 1979) that the sequences of momentary equilibria which satisfy (1.2), (1.3), and (1.4) may have catastrophic outcomes: only one such sequence is socially optimal, but they all satisfy short-run efficiency conditions; as a result, competition with incomplete futures markets may allow society to pick a sequence of momentary equilibria which involves excessive resource consumption with no warning being given by the price system. As we shall see, the pessimism of those authors may be exaggerated.

With competition insuring that (1.3) holds, the supply of resource is $R = R(\mu, S)$, with

$$\partial R/\partial \mu = 1/(P' - \partial^2 C/\partial R^2) < 0;$$

$$\partial R/\partial S = (\partial^2 C/\partial R\partial S)/(P' - \partial^2 C/\partial R^2) > 0 \,[9].$$

The isoclines in Figure 1.1, noted $\Delta S = 0$ and $\Delta \mu = 0$, are derived from (1.2) and (1.4) with R given by (1.3). Their slope is obtained by totally differentiating (1.1.) and (1.4) to get

$$d\mu/dS|_{\Delta S = 0} = -\partial^2 C/\partial R\partial S > 0. \qquad (1.7)$$

$$d\mu/dS|_{\Delta \mu = 0} = \qquad\qquad\qquad\qquad\qquad (1.8)$$

$$-[\partial^2 C/\partial S^2 + (\partial^2 C/\partial R\partial S)\partial R/\partial S]/[r + (\partial^2 C/\partial R\partial S)\partial R/\partial \mu)]$$

$$= A(d\mu/dS|_{\Delta S = 0}) \quad \text{where}$$

$$A = [(P' - \partial^2 C/\partial R^2)\,(\partial^2 C/\partial S^2)/(\partial^2 C/\partial R\partial S)^2 + 1]/$$

$$[r(P' - \partial^2 C/\partial R^2)/(\partial^2 C/\partial R\partial S) + 1].$$

---

[9] Since $\partial^2 C/\partial R\partial S$ is negative under the assumption that marginal cost is lower, the higher are the reserves.

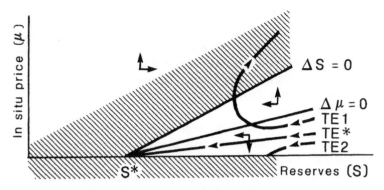

FIGURE 1.1 The dynamics of reserve stock and price in temporary equilibrium.

It is easily verified that $A < 1$; as a result, $d\mu/dS|_{\Delta\mu=0} < d\mu/dS|_{\Delta S=0}$ as represented in Figure 1.1[10].

In Figure 1.1, the direction of changes in S and μ on either sides of the isoclines are represented by horizontal and vertical arrows, respectively. Those are determined by checking the sign of the partial derivative of the right-hand side of (1.2) and (1.4) with respect to μ, still with R given by (1.3).

$$\partial(dS/dt)/\partial\mu = -\partial R/\partial\mu > 0$$

$$\partial(d\mu/dt)/\partial\mu = r + (\partial^2 C/\partial R\partial S)\,(\partial R/\partial\mu) > 0.$$

On any temporary equilibrium sequence, such as $TE1$ or $TE2$, S and μ move in the direction indicated by those arrows. It can be seen that only one such sequence leads to the steady state equilibrium. Since this equilibrium is also a necessary condition for optimality, it follows that all temporary equilibrium sequences other than TE^* are suboptimal.

Stiglitz, Dasgupta, and Heal have argued on those grounds that perfect competition without future markets, although it implies efficiency in the short run, is not likely to lead to efficiency in the long run. Quite the contrary, catastrophic mistakes are to be expected. A closer look at Figure 1.1 does not corroborate such an alarmist view.

---

[10] The case where $\Delta\mu$ has a negative slope is easily ruled out; it implies that it is optimal to leave valuable resources in the ground for ever, or that valuable resources are given a negative price.

First note that even in the most hopelessly myopic world, the hatched regions in Figure 1.1 are ruled out: the region above $\Delta S = 0$ because, there, S is increasing as if oil were pumped back into the ground; all other hatched regions because they involve negative values for either S or μ. This leaves only two types of erroneous temporary equilibrium sequences: that illustrated by $TE1$ and that illustrated by $TE2$. Suppose the myopic economy is on $TE1$. It follows that path until it gets some unambiguous indication to do otherwise. This message arrives when $TE1$ is about to cross the $\Delta S = 0$ isocline: continuing on along $TE1$ would involve negative extraction. Since S is higher than S^* at that point, the remaining reserves are still worth extracting, minimum average cost being below price, and people realize that μ had been too high. A downward revision puts the economy on a path closer to TE^*; no catastrophe has occurred and the cost of the mistake is simply to have been too conservative over a period. Suppose now that the myopic economy operates along $TE2$ instead. Here, a warning occurs when the path reaches the horizontal axis, so that μ is about to become negative. Again, at that point, S is higher than S^*; anybody realizes that it is inadequate to observe a price of zero for reserves that can be extracted at a cost which is below price. Somehow μ is revised upward and the economy continues on along some new path above $TE2$. No catastrophe has occurred in the sense that the warning was given before reserves were depleted; the cost of the mistake was to use the resource too thriftlessly over some period.

Why does this analysis lead to far less pessimistic an interpretation than earlier ones? This is yet another aspect of the Ricardian–Hotelling dichotomy. The case which was just examined is the Ricardian version of the general model. A similar analysis for Hotelling's polar case shows that the myopic economy does not receive any unambiguous warning until reserves are exhausted[11]. This holds true for simple one-factor models such as the one used here; it remains true in models involving substitution of capital for the resource as the later becomes more scarce (Dasgupta and Heal, 1979, chapter 8). To conclude, the absence of a complete set of future markets may be more damaging in the case of exhaustible resources than when the allocation of other

---

[11] The analysis is slightly different as exhaustion does not occur as a steady state equilibrium in the Hotelling case.

durable goods is concerned. This is more likely to be the case when the resource is highly homogeneous (Hotelling type) than when it occurs in a variety of qualities (Ricardian type) because suboptimal sequences of temporary equilibria may go undetected in the former case until the resource has been exhausted. Even then, as Solow (1974a) has pointed out, the type of myopia which causes this result is so extreme that it needs to be qualified. In reality economic agents do observe other indicators than prices; excessive rates of depletion are likely to be detected, and μ to be adjusted accordingly, before their consequences become too serious. Solow used the very instability of resource markets as another argument in favour of his moderate interpretation. He pointed out to the instability of the market for resource flows, the market which was assumed to be in (temporary) equilibrium in the above analysis. Indeed suppose that p does not rise fast enough so that (1.5) and, equivalently, (1.2) are out of equilibrium. Holders of reserves want to get rid of an asset which produces insufficient capital gains; by selling more of the resource, they deplete the price, further aggravating the temporary disequilibrium. Such a runaway from resources is enough of a signal for not-so-myopic agents to realize that μ had been overvalued in the previous temporary equilibrium sequence and to write off part of their reserves as capital losses: the revision that was called for in the extraction programme thus occurs before such a signal as extraction stoppage is observed.

In fact such adjustments, which break the sequence of temporary equilibria, may be one of the reasons why empirical verifications of Hotelling's price rule and its variants have not been very conclusive (Chapter 2). While central to the operation of any market involving valuable durable and storable goods, they are largely determined by market anticipations. Indeed as Salant and Henderson (1978), and Salant (1983), have shown, this is why attempts to control prices on such markets are vulnerable to speculative attacks.

1.9. Other imperfections

With the above qualifications, the absence of perfect futures markets has been shown to cause problems in resource sectors. This market incompleteness should not lead one to ignore other types of market imperfections encountered in the exploitation of non-renewable resources. Some occur because property rights are imperfectly defined.

For example some oil deposits are jointly owned by many agents. This
has caused problems of too rapid extraction in Texas and California,
and required public regulation. Property rights problems are not
limited to known reserves. The allocation of exploration rights, and
the extent to which subsequent reserves belong to their discoverers,
raise complex issues with both allocative and distributive implications.
Since the solution of those problems usually involves public intervention, they are exacerbated in areas where jurisdictional rights are
poorly or incompletely defined, such as the oceans and space, and
when particular information difficulties arise, as when extraction is
accompanied by pollution, or when costly exploration information
cannot be appropriated readily.[12]

1.10. Growth and survival

If scarcity types, i.e. the mix of Ricardian and Hotelling characteristics, affect the consequences of mistakes in resource management,
it should not come as a surprise that the future of our economies
depends on both their type of resource endowment and the way they
utilize them. This has led some authors to investigate such notions as
the importance of resources, and their role in the growth and survival
of an economy. Some resources such as energy are clearly essential;
the disappearance of some others may go almost unnoticed. While
oil is a very important commodity it is clearly not indispensable as
humanity has lived without it for most of its existence. Let aggregate
output Y be defined by the production function $G(L, K, R, X)$, where
L and K represent the services of capital and labour, respectively,
while, as before, R represents the flow of resource used as input in
aggregate production. X is a variable which accounts for Ricardian
characteristics of the resource: as cumulated extraction increases, extraction costs rise so that net aggregate output is reduced. Here, for analytical
convenience, X is defined as the inverse of cumulated extraction

$$X(t) = 1 / \int_{o}^{t} R(s)ds, \tag{1.9}$$

---

[12] For general, but more detailed, treatments of those issues, see Eswaran and Lewis
(1984a), the appropriate chapters in Fisher (1981), or Hartwick and Oleweiler (1986);
for an emphasis on risk and uncertainty, see Dasgupta (1982); for an emphasis on
environmental issues, see Tietenberg (1985), Kneese (1984), Johanson (1987). On the role
of information in exploration, see Dodds and Bishop (1983).

so it can be interpreted as a stock input whose level tends to zero if cumulated extraction tends to infinity; $\partial G/\partial X \geq 0$, with equality in the pure Hotelling case.

If $G(L, K, O, X) > 0$, the resource may be useful, but it is not necessary for production. This may represent the case of copper and oil, but probably not that of energy in general, nor that of water. So assume $G(L, K, O, X) = 0$ in order to focus on the most important and difficult cases. Since this is an aggregate technology, zero production actually means death; so it is reasonable to assume that society will be willing to pay a very high price for the marginal unit of resource when R is close to zero: the value of $\partial G(L, K, O, X)/\partial R$ is infinite. For the Ricardian model of resources, this implies that price will always meet extraction costs. If the resource is available in infinite supply, an important issue becomes whether extraction costs rise at a low enough rate that the economy is able to substitute capital for the resource in such a way as to maintain a non-vanishing level of consumption when X tends to zero. If the resource stock is finite, it is not optimal to leave any amount of it in the ground (the economy has Hotelling's characteristics). But since the resource is necessary for production, it is not optimal to exhaust it in any finite period. Again the question is whether it is possible for the economy to substitute capital for the resource in such a way that consumption of the finite stock can be spread over an infinite period while maintaining a non-trivial consumption level forever.

As Dasgupta and Heal (1979, p. 199) have argued, the simplest laboratory in which to explore such questions is the CES production function[13]

$$G(L, K, R, X) = \{\beta_1 f(L, K, R)^\pi + \beta_2 X^\pi\}^{1/\pi}$$

where $\pi = (\sigma_x - 1)/\sigma_x$, σ_x being the elasticity of substitution between the input aggregator $f(L, K, R)$ and X, while β_1 and β_2 must be non-negative and sum to one. This formulation can be interpreted as follows. Net output $Y = G(\cdot)$ is obtained by allocating some of L, K and R to aggregate production and the rest to the production of R; given a target level of R the quantity of inputs devoted to its production

---

[13] Kemp, Long, and Shimomura (1984) approach the issue of survival without parameterizing the technology, and with several resources, non-nul extraction costs, and technological change. Kemp and Long (1984b) extend the analysis to account for situations where a country does not have control of the finite resource stock.

depends on the level of X: the lower X (i.e. the higher cumulated extraction), the more inputs are necessary for resource production, and the higher the cost. In that sense, a drop in X can be interpreted as degradation at the Ricardian margin; the easiness with which this degradation can be offset by increases in the use of other inputs is measured by σ_x. It is reasonable to assume that σ_x is smaller than unity because, otherwise, it is possible to produce a strictly positive output without using any amount of L, K, or R, provided X is strictly positive[14]. Besides substitution at the Ricardian margin, which may help maintain the level of R, inputs can be substituted for R and R can be allowed to diminish. Because the cost or quality of R are irrelevant to this second type of adjustment, it can be recognized to represent a substitution at the Hotelling margin. Its easiness depends on substitution elasticities within $f(\cdot)$.

As a particular case, if $\beta_2 = 0$, then $G(\cdot) \equiv f(\cdot)$; if furthermore S is finite so that X must always exceed a strictly positive level $\underline{X}$, *we have the pure Hotelling case* which has been analyzed by Dasgupta and Heal (1979), following Solow (1974b) and Stiglitz (1974b). They take $f(\cdot)$ to be a linearly homogeneous C.E.S. function

$$f(L, K, R) = \{\alpha_1 K^\eta + \alpha_2 R^\eta + \alpha_3 L^\eta\}^{1/\eta}$$

where $\eta = (\sigma_R - 1)/\sigma_R$, σ_R being the elasticity of substitution between K and R; $\alpha_i > 0$, $\Sigma\alpha_i = 1$. Normalizing L to one, one has

$$F(K, R) = \{\alpha_1 K^\eta + \alpha_2 R^\eta + \alpha_3\}^{1/\eta}. \tag{1.10}$$

If $\sigma_R > 1$, $F(K, 0) > 0$: the resource is not necessary for production. If $\sigma_R < 1$, the Hotelling economy is doomed[15]. It is not surprising that the ease with which capital can be substituted for resource flows determines the fate of the economy and the importance of the resource to its survival. What is more striking is the fact that the limiting case arises when the elasticity is one, when the technology is Cobb-Douglas[16]. Here again we have clear-cut results due to Solow: If α_1, the share of

[14] In fact if $\sigma_x \geq 1$, $f(\cdot)^\pi = 0$ when $f(\cdot) = 0$, so that $Y = \beta_2 X \geq 0$. This could represent the case of an amenity resource such as the environment in general, which can be depleted to help produce manufacturing goods, but also produces amenity services if left untouched.
[15] Indeed it can be shown in that case that productivity tends to a finite value as R tends toward zero; as a result production, hence consumption, must eventually decline to zero.
[16] For a defence of the Cobb-Douglas function in this context, see Kemp and Long (1980a)

capital in aggregate income, exceeds α_2, the share of the resource, the resource, although *necessary* for production, is not *essential* for survival of the economy. Capital can be substituted fast enough for production eventually to require only minute amounts of R in such a way as never to exhaust reserves. If instead $\alpha_2 > \alpha_1$, the economy is doomed. In fact casual empiricism suggests that the first alternative prevails: data on factor shares indicate that α_2 is about 5% while the share of capital is around 20%.

These optimistic results apply to Hotelling-type economies. However, aggregate resource economies have definite Ricardian characteristics and the use of lower quality resources constitute yet another way to alleviate resource constraints on production. Let us assume $\beta_2 > 0$ in order to consider this possibility. First, remember that if S is finite, we have a mixed Hotelling/Ricardian economy: although non-homogeneous, S will be exhausted completely. The problem turns out to be entirely similar to that of a pure Hotelling economy: survival is a matter of being able to produce a non-trivial amount of $F(\cdot)$ when R tends to zero. All the above results remain valid.

Consider the pure Ricardian case now, where S is infinite so that X tends to zero. By assumption, $\sigma_x \leq 1$. If $x < 1$, increases in $F(\cdot)$ will not be able to offset the fact that X tends to zero[17]. So the fact that the economy is Ricardian will not release it from the necessity to substitute K for R as in the Hotelling economy. This leaves $\sigma_x = 1$ as limiting case, which is investigated by Lasserre (1989) under the assumption that substitution of capital for resource flows at the Hotelling margin would not be sufficient to avoid disappearance of the economy. Through adjustment at the Ricardian margin, it turns out that the catastrophic outcome predicated under that assumption for the Hotelling economy can be avoided. A necessary and sufficient condition for survival in that case is

$$\beta_2 \leq \alpha_1 \beta_1. \tag{1.11}$$

This means that the share of resource stock services in aggregate income must not exceed the combined share of all other inputs, K, L, and R, times the proportion of capital in the expenditures on those inputs.

---

[17] In order to see this, write $G(\cdot)$ as $Y^\pi = \{\beta_1 F(K, R)^\pi + \beta_2 X^\pi\}$ and divide by X^π to get $(Y/X)^\pi = \beta_1 (X/F(K, R))^{-\pi} + \beta_2$, with $-\pi > 0$. It follows that, when X tends to zero, $\lim Y = \lim \beta_2^{1/\pi} X = 0$.

TABLE 1.1   Survival with Exhaustible Resources

Substitution of K for R	Share of K relative to R	Pure Hotelling Case S finite, $\beta_2 = 0$	Mixed Case S finite, $\beta_2 > 0$		Pure Ricardian Case S infinite, $\beta_2 > 0$	
			Substitution of other inputs for reserves			
			easy ($\sigma_X > 1$)	difficult ($\sigma_X < 1$)	$\sigma_X = 1$	easy ($\sigma_X > 1$)
Easy ($\sigma_R > 1$)	Irrelevant	RESOURCE NOT NECESSARY				
$\sigma_R = 1$	$\alpha_2 < \alpha_1$	Resource necessary but inessential		Resource necessary but inessential		
	$\alpha_2 \geq \alpha_1$	economy is doomed		economy is doomed		Res. inessent. if $\beta_2 < \alpha_1\beta_1$
Difficult ($\sigma_R < 1$)	Irrelevant					

Table 1.1 provides a recapitulation of survival conditions for a resource economy. Even if one abstracts from the cases where the resource is trivially non-necessary, it does not appear likely that resource constraints will cause our economies to disappear. Capital can be substituted for resource flows in aggregate production; capital can also be used to offset the rise in extraction costs in a Ricardian economy. Survival is certain if the elasticity of substitution exceeds unity on either of those two margins; the economy is doomed if elasticities are lower than unity on both margins; in the limiting Cobb-Douglas cases, survival is possible if either the share of expenditures on R, or the share of the rental cost of X, is not too high relative to the appropriate shares of capital[18]. This analysis has been carried out while abstracting from several important considerations. Among those are population growth and technological change. Here again intuition has been aided by Stiglitz (1974b)'s simplified analysis of the Cobb-Douglas, pure Hotelling, case: the rate of resource augmenting technological change at least must be equal to the rate of population growth times the share of natural resources.

1.11. Monopoly

Because nature restricts the number of supply sources of several non-renewable resources, and because it also imposes their location, thus making the entry game less sophisticated, market power is perhaps more likely to be observed in resource sectors than in other areas of economic activity. On the other hand, while no other source of oil is as cheaply accessible as Middle Eastern oil, several alternative deposits are available at higher costs, as in the Ricardian version of the theoretical model developed above. To this limitation to market power, one must add the stock nature of extractive resources: when a monopoly restricts supply in any given period, it raises the reserve stock it will hold during subsequent periods, which amounts to increasing its own supply over those periods. In that sense, a resource monopoly competes with itself over time.

---

[18] Data on aggregate shares suggest that those conditions are met. For the more complex Ricardian model introduced here, the presence of two margins makes the calculation of shares more difficult. In particular, since X is the inverse of cumulated extraction, it reflects the stock of existing and potential reserves. The calculation of its rental cost requires data on the value of that stock; for an attempt at evaluating it, see Boskin *et al.* (1985).

The detection of monopolistic behaviour is also more difficult in resource sectors: as shown above (1.3), competitive profit maximizing requires that price be higher than marginal cost by the amount of the resource rent. As a result (Pindyck, 1987; Cairns, 1990b), standard measures of market power such as the Lerner index have to be modified.

Attitudes toward monopolistic behaviour have also been somewhat different in the case of non-renewable resources. First monopolistic behaviour has often been adopted by nations rather than private companies. This is often considered socially more acceptable, especially when those nations belong to the Third World. Second, and more important, as a monopoly restricts supply, it may be perceived as an objective ally by conservationists. Finally, and somewhat in contradiction with the last argument, resource monopolists to some extent have been described as powerless because, as mentioned above, they have to compete with themselves over time. As will be shown now, some of those attitudes are based on misunderstandings.

The Ricardian/Hotelling dichotomy can be usefully carried over to the analysis of the resource monopoly. For simplicity however, I will follow the lead of Hotelling, choosing to assume nul or constant marginal extraction costs and further assuming that reserves are homogeneous and finite. Let the inverse demand be $p = P(R, t)$ and marginal revenue be $m = \partial[P(R, t)R]/\partial R = \gamma p$, where $\gamma = (1 - 1/\epsilon)$, ϵ being the elasticity of demand. For a monopoly which maximizes the present value of its net revenue stream $\int_0^T e^{-rt} P(R, t)Rdt$ subject to $\int_0^T R(t)dt \leq S(0)$

$$m = \mu^m \tag{1.12a}$$

and

$$(dm/dt)/m = r \tag{1.12b}$$

where μ^m is the resource rent, as determined by the monopoly. If, instead, the sector was competitive, the following special versions of (1.3) and (1.4) would have to hold

$$p = \mu^c \tag{1.13a}$$

and

$$(dp/dt)/p = r. \tag{1.13b}$$

Thus, for a monopoly, marginal revenue, rather than price, is set equal to the rent (plus marginal cost if the latter is non-nul); under both monopoly and competition rent rises at the rate of interest, but the monopoly rent is not equal to the competitive rent in general.

Combining (1.12b) with the definition of m

$$(dm/dt)/m = (dp/dt)/p + ((d\gamma/dt)/\gamma = r \qquad (1.14)$$

it follows that price rises at the same rate under monopoly and competition if $d\gamma/dt = 0$, i.e. if the elasticity of demand is constant. If it is constant over the whole demand schedule, then price and output are identical under both market structures because, of all possible price trajectories which follow an exponential path, only one will imply an extraction path which exactly uses up the resource stock when taken over an infinite period[19].

This paradoxical result — that, under some circumstances, a resource monopoly behaves like a competitive firm — is due to Stiglitz (1976). It has been widely accepted and often interpreted to mean that monopoly was perhaps less of a nuisance in resource sectors than in conventional activities. Recently, Gaudet and Lasserre (1988) have argued that this interpretation was in fact a misunderstanding and that the essence of monopoly behaviour, in extractive sectors like in others, was indeed to restrict supply, in a socially damaging fashion. They first point out that a conventional monopolistic firm also behaves like a competitive one if it faces an isoelastic demand curve and produces at zero cost up to the capacity limit imposed by the presence of a fixed input: this is the textbook case of a firm facing a vertical marginal cost curve. Then they argue that Stiglitz's monopoly is the dynamic analogue of this textbook case: the monopoly faces a fixed reserve stock which works as a capacity constraint over the whole extraction period. In comparison with the textbook case, the paradox is not that the monopoly behaves like a competitive sector when demand is isoelastic; the paradox is that this seems to occur as a very special case while it is very easy to find alternative demand configurations that produce the same result in the static

---

[19] Under both market structures the extraction programme lasts forever. Suppose to the contrary that reserves are exhausted after a finite period T. Because demand is isoelastic, price shoots up from a finite level to infinity at T, and so does marginal revenue. Thus, whether it is competitive or monopolistic, the firm could have achieved higher profits by keeping some reserves at T in order to take advantage of the higher price. This proves that there is no finite date at which it is optimal to exhaust.

analysis[20]. The explanation is simple: unlike its static textbook counter-part, the resource monopoly has the possibility to reallocate output over time within the limits of the overall reserve constraint. Facing an isoelastic demand, it cannot profit from doing so; but other demand configurations leave more opportunities. If anything, the resource monopoly has more possibilities to exercise market power than the conventional firm.

It is when marginal cost rises with output that monopoly and competition differ in a rich fashion. Gaudet and Lasserre go on to argue that, for Stiglitz's model, rising marginal cost may be interpreted to mean that it is more expensive to acquire large amounts of reserves than small amounts. Once endowed with the possibility to choose an initial reserve stock, the resource monopoly turns out to pick a lower quantity than a competitive firm facing identical constraints. This is true whether $S(0)$ is the result of previous exploration activities or otherwise acquired. The resource monopoly has the restrictive behaviour that can be expected from any monopoly.

Solow (1977) gives additional insights into the reasons for a monopoly to explore less. One of them is that the monopoly can be viewed as having a sort of monopsony power on the exploration side: while both exploration by a monopoly and competitive exploration will reduce the rent, the monopoly, unlike the competitive firm, is aware of that effect and acts accordingly. Another reason arises when extraction costs are affected by the level of reserves, as in Pindyck (1978a, 1980). As a monopoly produces less, this cost effect will assume less importance.

1.12. Duopoly and oligopoly

The problems that have made dynamic industrial organization so challenging during the past 15 years were also at the core of theoretical research in resource economics. They include the adaptation to a dynamic context of concepts which were developed in a static frame-work, the Cournot–Nash duopoly and the Stackelberg duopoly in particular; they include efforts to tackle such issues as commitment

---

[20] The static monopoly with a vertical marginal cost curve may elect to produce less than a competitive firm under some demand configurations. Such is the case whenever the marginal revenue curve cuts the horizontal axis at a level which does not exceed the quantity at which the marginal cost curve becomes vertical.

and dynamic consistency; they also include the synthesis of work from various origins: the link between rational expectations and dynamic consistency, the link between sub-game perfectness in game theory, and closed-loop solution concepts in dynamic programming.

A landmark contribution in resource industrial organization is Salant's (1976) paper on duopoly. In an attempt to model the world oil market, Salant assumes that supply originates from two sources: a cartelized group of identical firms or countries on one hand and a fringe of identical competitive firms or countries on the other hand. All firms operate on a common market where demand chokes off when price exceeds p^{max}. The focus is not on technological or geophysical differences but on behavioural differences. Thus both sectors are assumed to hold homogeneous reserves of identical accessibility: marginal extraction cost will be taken to be zero in the version presented here.

The innovative part of the paper consists in treating the two sectors as a dynamic Cournot duopoly. Unlike the static counterpart, however, the two firms are not treated symmetrically: the competitive fringe takes the price as given and adjusts production accordingly; the cartelized sector sets the price and supplies whatever quantity is requested to meet demand, given the quantity supplied by the fringe. Both actors play simultaneously, while taking the decisions of their counterpart as given; thus the equilibrium is a Nash equilibrium. However, they do so while maximizing the present value of their profits, given their reserve constraint. As explained above for the competitive firm and for the monopoly, this imposes some constraints on the price trajectory over time. In fact if the competitive fringe is currently producing

$$(dp/dt)/p = r \qquad (1.13)b$$

and similarly for the cartel

$$(dm/dt)/m = r. \qquad (1.12)b$$

While those two dynamic constraints were developed and presented above as mutually exclusive alternatives, they must hold simultaneously in the duopoly case, as long as both sectors are in production. Another crucial difference with the monopoly case has to do with the definition of m. For the cartel, marginal revenue is defined on the residual demand, as opposed to the entire demand schedule. Indexing by '*c*' (competitive) and '*m*' (monopoly) the variables which are specific to the competitive fringe and the cartel, respectively, and assuming demand to be time autonomous, price is $P(R^c + R^m)$, residual revenue to the cartel is $R^m P(R^c + R^m)$, so that m is now defined as

$$m = P(R^c + R^m)\left[1 - 1/\epsilon^m\right]. \qquad (1.15)$$

In equilibrium, three alternative patterns of production may be envisaged: both types of firms produce simultaneously; the cartel produces alone, or the competitive fringe produces alone. Under all circumstances, the decision to produce, or not to produce, must be considered optimal by each type of firm. Thus when both types produce simultaneously, (1.12b) and (1.13b) must hold. When the competitive fringe is not producing but holds reserves, price must be rising at a faster rate than the discount rate: this makes it more profitable to hold on to reserves than to produce. This case is in fact ruled out because, if price was expected to rise at such a rate, speculative purchases would occur, causing the price to shoot up to a level where it could no longer be expected to rise that fast. When the competitive fringe is not producing because it has exhausted its resource, it must not be in a position to wish it had kept reserves instead: the price must not rise faster than the discount rate. Similarly, when the cartel is not in production, m, which is equal to price since $R^m = 0$, must not rise faster than the discount rate. Imposing those constraints on the alternative production configurations that can be envisaged, it can be shown that the sole possible pattern is one where the cartel and the fringe produce simultaneously in an initial phase, and the cartel produces alone in a final phase. As can be seen on Figure 1.2, the cartel's marginal revenue rises smoothly at the rate r over the whole period, as would be the case if a monopoly was alone on that market. However, m is defined on the residual demand, which differs from total demand over the first period. So there is a definite difference, which in fact is evident in the price trajectory: price rises at the rate r as long as the competitive fringe is in production, but rises at a lower rate once the cartel is alone on the market[21].

---

[21] If demand was isoelastic, p and m would rise at the same rate but exhaustion would not occur in a finite time for either the cartel or the fringe. In fact the first phase would last forever with the cartel and the fringe sharing a constant proportion of the market and behaving as a truly competive industry, i.e., for that matter, as a true monopoly.

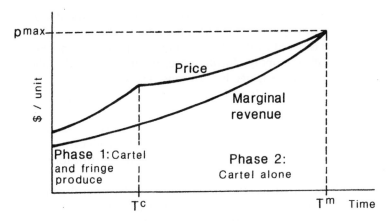

FIGURE 1.2 Price and marginal revenue in Salant's duopoly model.

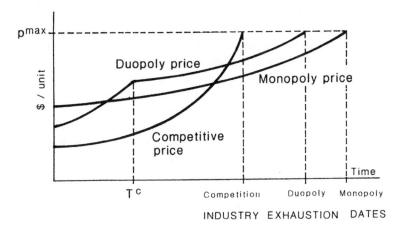

FIGURE 1.3 Price trajectories under competition, duopoly and monopoly.

In that equilibrium, the cartel, without purposely attempting to affect the quantities produced by the fringe, announces a price trajectory which induces the competitive fringe to produce, while leaving some of the demand for it to satisfy residually. At T^c, the cartel's market share has increased to one, so that there is no jump in m when it takes over completely in the second phase. As compared with the competitive, and the monopoly, equilibrium, Salant's duopoly lies inbetween (Figure 1.3).

Industry reserves last longer than under competitive exploitation, but exhaustion occurs earlier than under monopoly. The value of the firms in the cartel is raised by the exercise of market power, but not as much as under full monopoly; furthermore, as in many static oligopoly models, firms in the fringe benefit more from the cartelization than cartel members. This leaves industry structure unexplained theoretically, although, on heuristic grounds, it is thought that cartelization is more likely to occur when it yields high private benefits than otherwise. Pindyck (1978b) compared the gains from cartelization of several exhaustible resources and found empirical justification for this belief.

Salant's model can be generalized to firms with rising, although identical, marginal costs. It retains the empirically disturbing prediction that the cartel's market share increases over time until, in a final phase, it controls the totality of the market. Although it is clear that those results might not hold in a model with exploration and entry, one may wonder whether they are not produced by the assumption that all firms have identical costs. After all Middle Eastern oil is much cheaper than North Sea oil and the latter might have been in production before the creation of OPEC, had it been less expensive to extract. Another questionable feature of Salant's model is the use of a Nash concept of equilibrium. Is it realistic to assume that a cartel will take the quantity decisions of the competitive fringe as given?

Ulph (1982) studies a similar cartel model as Salant, but adds the assumption that firms have constant marginal costs, which differ in the fringe (C^c) and in the cartel (C^m). When extraction costs are sufficiently lower in the cartel and initial cartel reserves are sufficiently abundant, the following pattern arises: In an initial phase, the cartel is alone on the market and sets price and quantity in such a way that $m - C^m$ rises at the rate of interest[22]; $p - C^c$ rises at a lower rate and accordingly, the fringe is not producing. When the price reaches a certain level, it becomes optimal for the fringe to enter the market and this requires $p - C^c$ to start rising at the rate of discount, which is compatible with $m - C^m$ rising at the same rate if the share of the cartel diminishes over time. So in that second phase, both the cartel and the fringe produce simultaneously, with the fringe increasing its

---

[22] With constant marginal costs, p and m must be replaced by $p - C^c$ and $m - C^m$ respectively in (1.12b) and (2.13b).

market share. This goes on until the cartel exhausts its reserves and the fringe produces alone, at a competitive rate, in a last phase.

While this pattern is much more compatible with empirical evidence, there is another advantage to retaining the Nash concept of equilibrium in this context. If at each and any date, the programme is interrupted and the agents are allowed to reconsider their announced trajectories, they will stick to their initial decisions, and choose to continue the programme which was selected in the first place. In control language, the open loop (no revision) and the closed loop (perpetual revision) solution concepts give the same result for this problem. The equilibrium trajectories are dynamically consistent. In the language of game theory, the Nash equilibrium just described is also sub-game perfect: the two players are not committed to their announced strategies nor to the actions (price for the cartel or quantity for the fringe) that result from the implementation of those strategies. But given the opportunity to change their minds at any date, they maintain their earlier decisions. One reason for this intertemporal consistency is that their expectations are being fulfilled: if we think now of the relevant price and quantity trajectories as of expectations held by the parties, the values taken by those variables in equilibrium as time goes by are exactly the values which were expected in the first place; this is a rational expectations equilibrium.

In contrast, when Ulph examines the Stackelberg alternative as a behavioural assumption, he finds dynamic inconsistency in some configurations. In the Stackelberg model, the leader knows that the fringe reacts to his price decisions so that, instead of taking the fringe's output as given, he takes its determination into account when choosing a price trajectory. The result is not an equilibrium in price and quantity trajectories as in the case of the Cournot–Nash duopoly[23], but the solution of the following constrained optimization problem

$$\underset{R^m(t)}{Max} \quad \int_o^T e^{-rt} [P(R^{c^*}(t) + R^m(t)) - C^m] R^m(t)\, dt$$

[23] A Nash equilibrium is defined as a price trajectory selected by the cartel, and a quantity trajectory selected by the fringe, such that each of those trajectories is profit-maximizing for the group which selects it, given the other side's choice.

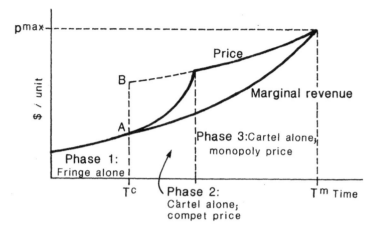

FIGURE 1.4 Price and marginal revenue of the cartel: Ulph's Stackelberg model.

subject to

$$\int_o^T R^m(t)\,dt \le S_o^m$$

$$R^{c*}(t) \text{ solves } \{Max \int_o^T e^{-rt}[p(t) - C^c]R^c(t)dt \,|\, \int_o^T R^c(t)dt \le S_o^c\}$$

$$p(t) = P(R^{c*}(t) + R^m(t))$$

When C^c is sufficiently small relative to C^m and S_o^c sufficiently abundant, Ulph finds the solution to involve three phases (Figure 1.4). In the first one, the fringe produces alone and $p - C^c$ rises at the discount rate. In the second phase, the fringe has exhausted its reserves and the cartel takes over while maintaining a price policy which is a continuation of the trajectory followed in the first phase. Finally, in the last phase, the cartel adopts the pricing policy that his monopoly position on the market justifies: $m - C^m$ rises at the discount rate. Why does not the cartel adopt monopoly pricing as soon as the fringe has exhausted its reserves, at the beginning of phase 2? Because that would involve an upward jump in price, from A to B. Knowing that the price was going to jump, the firms in the fringe would not produce as described in phase 1 because they had rather keep some reserves in order to take advantage of the price rise at T^c. In order to induce them into exhausting early, the cartel must announce that the price trajectory of phase 2 will indeed be followed. But is this credible? Once the fringe has exhausted its reserves, nothing prevents the cartel from acting in its best interest, which is to adopt the monopoly price immediately. The solution devised at time zero is dynamically inconsistent, in the sense that it will not be continued if it is allowed to be revised during its application. Since it is not in his interest to stick to it once it has eliminated the competitive fringe, the price trajectory announced by the cartel is not credible. This is how the issue of commitment, common in game theory, also arises in the non-game-theoretic framework of the Stackelberg resource duopoly.

Resource cartels were also studied, in particular, by Ulph and Folie (1980), and Lewis and Schmallensee (1980). Newberry (1981) addressed the problem of dynamic inconsistency more specifically, while Eswaran and Lewis (1984b) provided a good discussion on alternative behavioural assumptions in resource oligopolies. Reinganum and Stockey (1981) widened the strategy space by allowing threats and punishments to defectors while Loury (1986), under the assumption of precommitment (open loop strategies) generalized the analysis to n players. Understandably, his analysis has all participants play in quantities since it is no longer clear what could distinguish a cartel from the fringe when the number of non-cooperative players is high. Some interesting additional problems arise when a substitute to the resource can be introduced (Hoel, 1983; Dasgupta and Stiglitz, 1981) or when exploration and discoveries enter the picture (Hartwick and Sadorsky, 1989).

2. EMPIRICAL TESTS AND PRICE STUDIES

2.1. Reminder

At the basis of natural resource economics is the treatment of exhaustible reserves as assets. Resource prices and flows must be selected in such a way as to simultaneously equilibrate the market for resource flows and the (possibly implicit) market for reserves. As is too obvious from the previous section, that principle underlies a multiplicity of models, which in turn generate a multiplicity of predictions. This makes it extremely difficult unambiguously to test the underlying principle, as opposed to alternative features of the models built around it.

As most tests involve resource prices, a reminder of the major theoretical predictions in that respect is appropriate. Hotelling's simplest model calls for a steady rise in the net price of non-renewable resources, with interest rate being the central determinant of the growth rate. While this result holds with only slight modifications under alternative market structures, it is seriously affected when a number of important and empirically relevant complicating factors are taken into account. The price does not rise as fast when the resource is heterogeneous; U-shaped price trajectories and other patterns may arise in presence of exploration, technological change, or delays in capacity build-up, as well as changes in demand over time. In a world involving uncertainty, various forms of Hotelling rule arise, depending on the stochastic processes and the variables affected by them. While the stochastic rule is sometimes simply a version of its non-stochastic counterpart written in terms of expected values (Deshmukh and Pliska, 1980; Slade, 1988), the presence of uncertainty usually introduces complications of a much larger magnitude[24] (Pindyck, 1980; Arrow and Chiang, 1982; Lasserre, 1984a; Quyen,1988). For those reasons, while most empirical studies in that area present themselves as tests of the Hotelling principle, they are rightly interpreted as attempts to identify the relevant empirical variables and specification for the purpose of resource price modelling, within the capital theoretic framework of Hotelling, rather than being interpreted as tests of that theory.

Besides the relevance of the capital theoretic approach to natural resource economics, Hotelling rule has been interpreted as a statement about resource scarcity. The rise in rent is indicative of rising scarcity, which is the empirical fact needing to be tested. Indeed, one of the best known early empirical studies of resources (Barnett and Morse, 1963) focuses on scarcity rather than prices *per se*. Moreover, it is based on a purely Ricardian view, implying that scarcity arises from increases in extraction costs rather than exhaustibility. The authors use two alternative measures of Ricardian scarcity: absolute productivity of

---

[24] Several empirical studies (for example Heal and Barrow, 1980; Smith, 1979; Slade, 1982; Hall and Hall, 1984) assume either implicitly or explicitly that under uncertainty the expected rate of increase of net resource price must equal the expected rate of interest.

either labour or labour and capital; and productivity in extractive sectors relative to productivity in manufacturing sectors. Within the long-run focus of their study which was based on US data for 1870–1957, they do not find any statistical support for the hypothesis of rising scarcity. In some instances, Americans have transmitted increased (lower cost) resources to subsequent generations, and productivity of extractive sectors has kept pace with productivity in manufacturing industries. If one focuses on the most recent years in their first study period, this conclusion is perhaps less solidly founded. So the study was updated (Barnett, 1979) to include the 1958–1973 period and the data base was enlarged to cover several OECD countries besides the United States. For several sectors, a change in the long-run trend seems to be occurring in the most recent years of the data base, although the new trend remains statistically insignificant.

While Barnett and Morse's study was interpreted by many as a dismissal of Hotelling's theory, other resource economists were quick to point out that it bore little relationship with that theory. Indeed, in the pure version of Hotelling's model, costs (and productivity) are constant but a scarcity rent drives a wedge between price and marginal cost. What ought to be tested is the presence of scarcity rents, as well as the behaviour of rents and prices over time.

2.2. Evidence on scarcity rents

The existence of rents is fairly well documented for the oil and gas industry over the last two decades. While extraction costs in the Persian Gulf region often do not exceed a few dollars for oil which is never sold below 12 dollars and has often reaped a price in the 30 dollar range, rents are also identified in other oil producing areas of the world. Even if, as argued by Devarajan and Fisher (1982), some of those rents simply remunerate previous exploration activities, rents have been shown by Lasserre (1985b) to exist on unexplored land. However, it is not clear at all that those rents are indeed scarcity rents; as argued, among others, by Pindyck (1987), much heuristic evidence suggests that they probably include a substantial monopoly component.

The evidence is even more controversial in non-oil sectors. Stollery (1983) tested the existence of resource rents in the Canadian nickel industry, after correcting for the non-competitive structure of that sector. While he found significant resource rents, his model was too crude[25] not to be open to alternative interpretations. Cairns (1986), whose own early estimations had led him to conclude that rents were negligible (Cairns, 1981) convincingly argued that Stollery's results were also consistent with a myopic model of mark-up pricing by nickel firms. In order to limit the scope for alternative interpretations, it became clear that more sophisticated models of the technology had to be tested. Besides the mere presence of rents, those models also investigated the compatibility of price and rent paths with the theory of natural resources.

2.3. Evidence on the behaviour of rents and prices over time

Smith (1979) studies a wide range of resource prices while controlling for such important factors as extraction costs, new discoveries, changes in market structure, and changes in the institutional environment. He finds little evidence to back Hotelling-type models and concludes that simple time series models have the best predictive power. Slade (1982), however, argues that declining price-path can be explained by technological change. Her model implies that the scarcity component in the equation describing the price path will eventually become dominant and cause the price to rise. Under sensible assumptions, this implies convex, rather than linear price trajectories. She successfully tested this property for several metals. More recently, Slade (1988) reverted to a position which is closer to that of Smith. Although the focus of her paper is grade selection rather than prices *per se*, she provides evidence that long-run copper prices appear to be generated by a martingale rather than by a process involving a rising component due to Hotelling scarcity.

Smith also devotes considerable attention to another aspect of resource price formation, which was first studied by Heal and Barrow (1980). Those authors argue that resource pricing is affected by arbitrage in asset markets, and that those markets may not exhibit the full information equilibrium assumed by simple models. In their empirical work, they find confirmation that changes in interest rates, more than their level, are important in determining metal price

---

[25] For example, Stollery used heroic assumptions to measure marginal extraction costs in a very secretive industry.

movements. This can be rationalized if there is uncertainty about future prices of resources relative to other assets. Although the supply side of their model is remote from Hotelling's—it does not take account of the depletable nature of resources—they interpret their results to confirm the importance of capital theoretic considerations in the formation of resource prices. Capital theoretic aspects, they argue, extend to other assets and, for that reason, resource prices may be expected to exhibit movements that are more complicated than the partial equilibrium model of Hotelling predicts. In a later paper, Heal and Barrow (1981) include proxies for resource depletion and cost changes, so that they claim that the simple version of the Hotelling model is nested within their model, and is rejected.

A better theoretical foundation for their model is perhaps to be found in the recent work of Gaudet and Khadr (1991) and Gaudet and Howitt (1989) who present a two-good capital-asset-pricing model of resource extraction and capital investment involving an explicit allocation of assets between resources and other types of capital, with production uncertainty in both the extractive and the non-extractive sectors. In both models, there exists a third asset with the characteristics of a risk-free bond, which yields the risk-free return r, and the solution is derived in general equilibrium. It is shown that the rate of increase of the net resource price must be more or less than the rate of interest, depending upon whether it is negatively or positively correlated with the marginal utility of consumption. These models have not been tested, however, although the authors provide clues on the way to go about it.

Another group of economists have taken a diametrically different approach to the objective of testing time consistency in resource prices or rents. Their emphasis is on the supply side, and they use a partial equilibrium framework, without any consideration for the pool of alternative assets which may affect demand. Farrow (1985), Halvorsen and Smith (1987), and Dea et al. (1988) adapt modern factor demand estimation methods to resource firms. From cost, production, factor utilization, and reserve data, it is possible to estimate a restricted cost function, from which the shadow price of in situ resources (the rent) can be computed, using the fact that the latter is related to the effect of reserves, or cumulated extraction, on marginal extraction cost. The appropriate version of equation (1.4)

$$d\mu/dt = r\mu + \partial C(R, S)/\partial S, \qquad (1.4)$$

provides a test of the theory of natural resources. In fact, if μ is computed from (1.3) using the estimated value of $\partial C/\partial R$

$$p = \partial C(R, S)/\partial R + \mu \qquad (1.3)$$

and $d\mu/dt$ is approximated as the variation in μ from one observation to the next one, (1.4) can be expressed entirely in terms of estimated parameters and observed variables, so that it can be tested as an additional constraint to the estimation of the cost function. While each paper uses a different variant of that procedure, and applies it to different data set (aggregate nonferrous metal mines in Canada in the case of Halvorsen and Smith; Canadian asbestos in the case of Dea *et al.*; confidential single mining company data in the case of Farrow), they all reject the hypothesis that the firms behave according to (1.4), as implied by the non-stochastic theory of natural resources. In this vein of empirical investigation too, it seems that the next step is to connect the resource asset with the rest of the portfolio in the economy and to test the corresponding more sophisticated, and stochastic, pricing rule.

Miller and Upton (1985) also test the theory of exhaustible resources using estimates of the *in situ* prices of a resource. However, instead of using time-series data on resource prices, they use panel data on asset prices to test what they refer to as the Hotelling Valuation principle. They exploit the fact, noted above, that both the asset market for reserves, and the market for resource flows, must be in equilibrium. Indeed, if resource price are expected to rise according to Hotelling rule, then the value of current reserves will be proportional to current resource prices, net of extraction costs, times reserve size. According to Tobin's q theory, this value will be reflected in the prices of firm stocks, which provides the basis of Miller and Upton's test equation.

$$V^i(t)/S^i(t) = \alpha + \beta[p^i(t) - \partial C^i/\partial R^i]$$

where $V^i(t)$ is the total market value of firm i at t and C^i is evaluated at t. From the fact that this equation is a better predictor of share prices for oil and gas firms in the US than alternative share valuation methods, the authors find a confirmation of Hotelling's theory. The difference in methodology with previously described tests is also revealing. The authors of those tests attempted to check whether resource price paths conformed to a certainty version, or a certainty analogue, of Hotelling rule. They do not appear to do so. This may imply that the theory of natural resource does not have any role in the determination of resource price behaviour; it may also imply that the appropriate stochastic version of that theory is not to be formulated in terms of expected prices and that, if it can be formulated in terms of expected prices, the formation of expectations must be given proper attention. Indeed, using a simple model of lagged expectations formation, Agbeyegbe (1989) rationalizes Barrow and Heal's finding that metal prices appear to be determined by changes in the interest rate rather than its level.

Despite the existence of a substantial body of empirical literature on the theory of natural resources, as it has evolved from the basic contribution of Hotelling, its empirical validity still remains an open question, which will not be resolved overnight. Apparently conflicting results probably reflect the use of highly simplified formulations of the theory, and the resulting focus of most authors on very partial explanations of the evidence. Cairns (1990a) offers a careful discussion which aims at reconciling several apparent contradictions in that literature . . . before providing his own additional, and mixed, evidence on Canadian gold mines.

3. JOINT PRODUCTS AND THE ENVIRONMENT

3.1. Introduction

Joint production is a frequent occurrence in natural resource industries. In one type of instance, pollution is produced jointly with the desirable product. For example, mine concentrators are often heavy water polluters while smelters are responsible for various emissions into the atmosphere. In another type of instance, several metals coexist in the same ore, each facing a specific demand. In fact many Canadian copper mines would not be in operation if it were not for the gold which is recuperated from the same ore. But the associated product may also face a weak demand and be simply discarded. This is what happens to some of the helium associated with American natural gas. Helium may become a highly valuable product in the future; should something be done about it? The physical nature of the products must also be taken into account when studying joint products. Some, such as noise, are pure flows. Some, such as gold, are perfect durable goods. Some, such as helium, can be released into the atmosphere at no cost, but can also be stored for future demand. Finally, several pollutants are stocks which build up in the atmosphere, on land, or in the water. Here it is worthwhile noticing that the problem of optimally accumulating an undesirable stock is very similar to the problem of the mine, which is optimally to deplete a valuable stock. Principles of public finance, basic capital theory, and the theory of the mine can be applied, together or alternatively, in order to highlight the issues and study the answers. One set of issues is purely positive: how should the conventional model of the mine be adapted for joint production? What is the rent on an individual resource in composite ore? Should the net price of individual resources rise at the interest rate? To what extent may a high demand for one resource cause another one to be wasted and is there any link between the prices of the resources being produced from the same ore? The other issue is normative. Should goverment intervene in some instances of joint production and how? Should clean-up activities or pollution abatement efforts be promoted and how? Does the fact that pollution is often a transnational externality affect the analysis?

3.2. Joint production from composite reserves

Pindyck (1982) provides a treatment of the joint production from composite ores problem. He uses the example of helium, jointly produced with natural gas, to motivate his paper. Markets are assumed competitive everywhere. There are two production stages. First, the composite ore is extracted at an average and marginal cost $MC(S)$ which depends on existing reserves only. Second, the individual resources are separated out from the ore at a cost $C^i(y^i, R)$ which depends, for each individual component i, on the rate of production y^i and on current extraction R of composite ore. The following reasonable assumptions are made: $\partial C^i/\partial y > 0$, $\partial^2 C^i/\partial y^{i2} > 0$, $\partial C^i/\partial R < 0$, $\partial^2 C^i/\partial R^2 > 0$, $\partial^2 C^i/\partial y^i \partial R < 0$, $\partial (C^i/R)/\partial R > 0$, $C^i(0, R) = 0$, and $C^i(y^i, 0) = \infty$.

With a^i and b^i respectively designating the unit cost of storage and the quantity stored for good i, and with p^i and q^i designating price and quantity of good i sold, the problem of the competitive firm is to choose $R, y^1, \ldots, y^n, q^1, \ldots, q^n$ in such a way as to

$$Max \int_0^\infty e^{-rt}\left[\sum_i p^i q^i - MC(S)R - \sum_i C^i(y^i, R) - \sum_i a^i b^i\right]dt$$
(3.1)

subject to

$$dS/dt = -R, \; S(0) = S_0$$

$$db^i/dt = y^i - q^i, \; b^i(0) = 0, \; i = 1, \ldots, n$$

$$S, R, y^i, q^i, b^i \geq 0, \; i = 1, \ldots, n$$

Since the industry is assumed competitive, all prices are treated as given in the maximization but in the industry equilibrium $p^i = p^i \, (q^i)$, $i = 1, \ldots, n$. This problem is only slightly more complicated than the problem of the single resource mine treated earlier. The major difference is not so much the summations over n resources in the objective function as the presence of a two-stage production process. What was considered the output of the firm in our earlier treatment is only a composite ore which still needs to be separated out in Pindyck's problem. As will become clear presently, the analog of the market price in the earlier problem is in fact here the transfer price for extracted ore. The Hamilton–Lagrange function is

$$H = e^{-rt}\left[\sum_i p^i q^i - MC(S)R - \sum_i C^i(y^i, R) - \sum_i a^i b^i \right.$$
(3.2)

$$\left. - \mu R + \sum_i \lambda^i(y^i - q^i) + \sum_i \Theta^i b^i\right]$$

with $\Theta^i = 0$ if $b^i < 0$, $\Theta^i \geq 0$ if $b^i = 0$. As before the Lagrange multipliers Θ^i and costate variables m and λ^i are expressed in current value.

Maximizing the Hamiltonian with respect to R gives

$$\mu = -\left[\sum_i \partial C^i/\partial R + MC(S)\right]$$

$$\mu = [p - MC(S)]$$
(3.3)

where $p \equiv -\Sigma_i \partial C^i/\partial R$ is the transfer price for extracted ore. Thus the rent can still be viewed as the difference between price and marginal cost of extraction, provided the appropriate transfer price is used. Why can p be interpreted as a transfer price? It represents the joint value to the separation departments, in terms of cost savings, of the marginal unit of extracted ore. Differentiating (3.3) with respect to time

$$d\mu/dt = dp/dt - (\partial MC/\partial S)(dS/dt).$$

Combined with the necessary condition $d\mu/dt = r\mu - e^{rt}(\partial H/\partial S)$, this gives

$$dp/dt = r(p - MC(S)) \tag{3.4}$$

which is the analog of (1.5) under the current assumptions on the extraction cost function. Looking now at the separation and storage phase, we have the following first-order conditions for a maximum with respect to y^i and q^i

$$-\partial C^i/\partial y^i + \lambda^i = 0, \, i = 1, \ldots, n \tag{3.5}$$

$$p^i - \lambda^i = 0, \, i = 1, \ldots, n \tag{3.6}$$

so that

$$p^i = \partial C^i(y^i, R)/\partial y^i. \tag{3.7}$$

The price of each resource is equal to its marginal production cost, given the optimal input of ore. This may appear in contrast with the previous result on the single-resource mine, (1.3), according to which price was equal to marginal cost plus rent. But again, this is now the second phase of the extraction-separation process. A fictive transfer price p has been paid for the extracted ore, and $C^i(y^i, R)$ is the variable cost function of product i, conditional on the fixed factor R. In (1.3), μ drives a wedge between price and marginal cost because R is the rate of output in the relevant cost function. There is no such wedge in (3.7) because R is fixed and marginal cost is defined on variations in y^i instead. The minimization by choice of R of the total cost of producing i, which is the sum of variable cost $C^i(y^i, R)$ and fixed cost $\mu^i R$, requires

$$\mu^i = -\partial C^i/\partial R. \tag{3.8}$$

This provides an evaluation of μ^i An alternative evaluation of μ^i is obtained by starting from the total cost of producing all n resources

$$TC = \sum_j C^j(y^j, R) + MC(S)R. \qquad (3.9)$$

The marginal cost of producing resource i is

$$\partial TC/\partial y^i = \partial C^i/\partial y^i + \left\{ \sum_j (\partial C^j/\partial R)\partial R/\partial y^i \right\} + MS(S)\partial R/\partial y^i$$

$$= p^i + (\partial R/\partial y^i)\left[\left\{ \sum_j (\partial C^j/\partial R)\right\} + MC(S)\right]$$

$$= p^i - (\partial R/\partial y^i)[p - MC(S)] \qquad (3.10)$$

which yields the analog of (1.3)

$$p^i = MC^i + \mu^i \qquad (3.11)$$

where $MC^i \equiv \partial TC/\partial y^i$ and $\mu^i = (\partial R/\partial y^i)[p - MC(S)]$.

We now have the answer to some of the positive issues raised above. The rent on the composite ore is given by (3.3); the rent on any individual resource buried in composite ore is given in (3.11) or, alternatively, by (3.8). As far as the price paths, there is an analog to Hotelling rule, but it governs the transfer price of the extracted ore only. Indeed if the reserves are homogeneous, so that MC(S) is constant at MC, (3.6) implies that the net transfer price p - MC is rising at the rate of interest. But there is no general prediction concerning the time paths of individual resource prices.

For each i, differentiating (3.6) with respect to time and combining with the necessary condition giving the time path of λ^i, $d\lambda^i/dt = r\lambda^i - e^{rt}\partial H/\partial b^i$, one has the usual condition on the price of a storable good

$$dp^i/dt \le rp^i + a^i \qquad (3.12)$$

which holds with equality if $b^i > 0$[26]. This shows that the resource in low current demand will be stored only if its storage cost is low: if a^i is high, (3.12) cannot hold with equality with p^i remaining low.

---

[26] One notes the similarity between this expression and (3.4), the condition which must be satisfied by the price of a natural resource in equilibrium. A natural resource is a commodity stored underground at no cost, but which is costly to recover.

The description of the solution is completed by a set of transversality conditions which will not be repeated here. Pindyck also examines the extent to which the demand for one resource will affect the price behaviour of the other resources. He argues that this depends strongly on the availability and cost of storage. 'Consider a composite containing one resource in high demand (e.g. natural gas) and a second resource whose demand today is small but very inelastic, or is expected to be much larger in the future (e.g. helium). Suppose storage of the second resource is costly. Then, relative to what would prevail if they could be produced independently, jointness of production will reduce the current price of the second resource and speed up its exhaustion, and at the same time will raise the current price of the first resource and delay its exhaustion. The cheaper the cost of storage, the more this effect is reduced'.

The answer to the normative question of government intervention is also contained in the analysis just presented since, with minor changes, the latter can be interpreted as the search of a social optimum. Although some helium may be released in the atmosphere in the competitive equilibrium, this release will be optimal. Of course this conclusion does not apply if there is an externality attached to any of the jointly produced components as happens when one output, whether good or bad, does not have any market. In that case, there is a competitive, and a social, version of problem (3.1). Suppose that the instantaneous social welfare function is the sum of consumer surpluses on individual goods i

$$W(q^1, \ldots, q^n) = V^1(q^1) + \ldots + V^n(q^n), \text{ where}$$

$$V^i(q^i) = \int_0^{q^i} P_i(q^i) \, dq^i. \tag{3.13}$$

Substituting $V^i(q^i)$ for $p^i q^i$ in (3.1) gives the social version of the problem. In the absence of externalities, its solution is identical to the solution of the competitive extraction problem just outlined.

Suppose now that there is no market for good $n + 1$; the solution to the social problem is now different from the solution to the competitive problem. In fact, indexing variables by 's' for social and 'c' for competitive.

$$\mu^c = \left[p^c - MC(S^c) \right] \tag{3.3c}$$

where $p^c \equiv - \Sigma_{i=1}^{n} \partial C^i / \partial R$ is the transfer price for extracted ore in a competitive firm.

$$\mu^s = \left[p^s - MC(S^s) \right] \qquad (3.3s)$$

where $p^s \equiv - \Sigma_{i=1}^{n+1} \partial C^i / \partial R$ is the transfer price for extracted ore in a social optimization context. If good $n + 1$ is a non-appropriable good no cost is incurred in the private competitive set-up in order to produce it; thus p^c is defined over n goods. In a social welfare maximization context, society prefers to make it available and $\partial C^{n+1} / \partial R$ is the reduction in its production cost associated with a marginal increase in R. For any given level of S and R, $p^s > p^c$, so that $\mu^s > \mu^c$; but then the implied time trajectory of the transfer price, as given by the analog of (3.4), is also affected; the gap between p^c and p^s keeps rising, and if equalities (3.3c) and (3.3s) are to be maintained over time, R^c and R^s must follow different paths. This in turn affects the marginal production costs of all private goods. Despite the assumption that the production technologies are separable for all $n + 1$ goods ($\partial^2 C^i / \partial y^i \partial y^j = 0$), and that the analysis has been carried out in a partial equilibrium framework, all real variables are different in the socially optimal solution than in the private one. In this particular case it may be conjectured that, in the socially optimal solution, the higher transfer price is spread over a higher number of separation departments, so that the contribution of each one is lower than in the private setup. As a result the production of all private goods is increased. The opposite may be expected if the non-private product is a 'bad'. In order to implement the socially optimum solution, a government would need all the information required to set the right subsidized price trajectory for good $n + 1$. This includes all the $n + 1$ transformation technologies, the extraction technology, the n demand schedules for private goods, and the social welfare function attached to good $n + 1$.

3.3. Optimum pollution stocks and clean-up

Pindyck's model is adequate for the study of jointly produced goods which affect private or social welfare as flows. It has two weaknesses. First, in several instances of pollution, it is the stock of a particular component which matters. Think of the greenhouse effect or think of the saturation of ocean or inland dumping sites. Undesirable stocks build up as economic activity proceeds. They may be associated with activities unrelated to the exploitation of exhaustible resources, as happens with the production of domestic waste; or they may be associated with the use of exhaustible resources, as is to a wide extent the case when the consumption of energy adds to the greenhouse effect. Second, there are ways — pollution abatement and clean-up efforts — to reduce undesirable emissions or to control the growth of the undesirable stock. The model presented now clarifies those aspects of the problem and can easily be adapted to various special cases.

Society extracts a resource whose transformation or consumption releases a certain pollutant. A typical example is energy and air pollution. The pollution is cumulative; the damage stock D grows in proportion to the resource extraction rate, but can also be affected by various pollution control efforts e whose unit cost is w[27].

$$dD/dt = nR - e, \; e \geq 0; \; D(0) = D_o \text{ small.} \qquad (3.14)$$

The instantaneous social welfare function is $V(R) + U(-D)$ with V defined by (3.13) and U rising and concave, so that V' is the price of the resource and U' can be interpreted as the value to society of reducing the damage stock by one unit. For society, assuming zero extraction cost, the problem to solve by choice of R and e is

$$Max \int_0^T e^{-rt}[V(R) + U(-D) - we]dt \qquad (3.15)$$

subject to (3.14) and the usual exhaustibility and non-negativity constraints (1.2). The Hamiltonian is

$$H = e^{-rt}[V(R) + U(-D) - (w - \eta - \lambda)e - (\lambda n + \mu)R]$$

where η is the Lagrangian multiplier associated with the non-negativity constraint on e and $H(\cdot)$ has been written in such a way that λ, the costate variable associated with D, is non-negative and represents the social gain from a drop in D.

For a maximum the following necessary conditions must be satisfied

$$V'(R) = P(R) = \lambda n + \mu \qquad (3.16)$$

$$w = \eta + \lambda \qquad (3.17)$$

$$d\mu/dt = r\mu \qquad (3.18)$$

---

[27] It is not difficult to introduce nature's absorption capacity to the analysis; this can take the form of a constant, or a term proportional to D, being subtracted from (3.14).

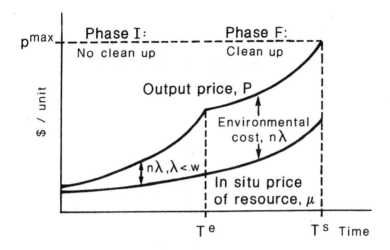

FIGURE 3.1 Socially optimal price and rent.

$$d\lambda/dt = r\lambda - U'. \qquad (3.19)$$

Two situations may arise (See Figure 3.1). If $\eta = 0$, so that $e \geq 0$, (3.17) implies that $\lambda = w$, which is assumed constant; (3.19) reduces to

$$U'(-D) = rw. \qquad (3.20)$$

which defines a constant level of damage D^{s*}. e is actually chosen so as to offset the polluting effect of resource extraction and consumption, in order to maintain the level of D at D^{s*}. Clearly this characterizes a situation where D has reached the level at which society is willing to devote control efforts to the prevention of further increases. This final phase (phase F) may be preceded by a situation where society does not find it necessary to check the growth of D; such initial phase (phase I) is observed if, as postulated above, $D_o < D^{s*}$. Thus n is positive, so that, by (3.17), $\lambda < w$, and $e = 0$; since $e = 0$, D is rising. This phase leads into phase F which begins when D reaches D^{s*} from below.

Under the assumption that demand chokes off at $p = p^{max}$, the socially optimal price of energy rises in such a way that (3.16) is maintained, while μ grows at the rate of interest. In the final (mature) phase, λ is constant at $\lambda = w$ (Phase F); but in the initial phase I, λ grows according to a modified Hotelling rule, (3.19). For example,

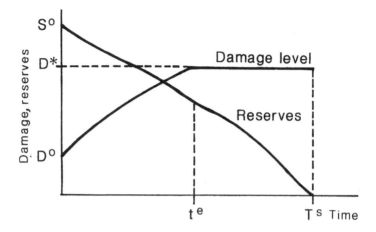

FIGURE 3.2 Socially optimal reserves and damage level.

such a rule should be expected to govern the price at dumping sites until treatment facilities are built and process domestic waste at unit cost w. Thus in phase F, p^s maintains a constant gap nw above the exponential curve μ^s, while in phase I this gap is smaller than nw and increases over time. T^s is the exhaustion date, and t^e signals the transition from phase I to phase F, when e becomes positive. These dates must be such that reserves are exactly exhausted over $[0, T^s]$; this is achieved by appropriate choice of $\mu^s(0)$. Figure 3.2 describes what happens to reserves and damage. During phase I, reserves diminish while damage increases, with $e = 0$; during phase F, reserves still diminish, but damage is maintained at D^{s*} by appropriate cleanup efforts. In the special case where there is no exhaustibility constraint as, perhaps, when the production of domestic waste is associated with general economic activity, the solution just described applies with $\mu = 0$ and S vanishing from the analysis; in the final phase, the price is constant.

Although highly simplified[28], this model confirms the general intuition that, while some pollution may be acceptable, society is willing to devote resources to clean up or prevent further damage when

---

[28] Plourde and Yeoung (1989) analyse a slightly more sophisticated model of industrial pollution in a stochastic environment.

pollution levels become high enough. It is interesting to compare the competitive outcome with the socially optimal solution just described. Under perfect competition, if pollution costs are not internalized, firms will solve the following problem

$$Max_R \int_o^T e^{-rt} pR dt \text{ subject to (1.2)} \qquad (3.21)$$

The solution must satisfy $p = \mu^c$ and $d\mu^c/dt = r\mu^c$, with $\mu^c(0)$ chosen so as to exactly exhaust reserves at T^c. Of course, in the competitive solution, D increases over the whole period $[0, T^c]$. It can also be shown that exhaustion occurs faster than is socially optimum as shown in Figure 3.3 where the competitive and socially optimal price and rent paths have been drawn on the same time scale[29]. Implementation of the social optimum not only requires an appropriate clean-up or abatement effort to be extended; it also requires the price of energy to be raised in order to slow its consumption.

The current period provides many instances of attempts to move toward social outcomes of the type just described, either through direct public intervention, or by creating institutions to implement those outcomes. Among the instruments that have been advocated or introduced are output and input taxes, regulations requiring certain pollution abatement equipment, tradable and non-tradable emission taxes and quotas, etc. (Buchanan and Tullock, 1975; Baumol and Oates, 1975; Tietenberg, 1985; Kneese, 1984; Johanson, 1987). Given the tremendous amount of information required to characterize the social

---

[29] In both cases, optimality requires that $p = p^{max}$ when exhaustion occurs. Suppose p^c was everywhere above p^s; at all dates prior to T^c R^s would be higher than R^c; then if at T^c reserves are exactly exhausted under the competitive price path, they must be more than exhausted under the socially optimum path. Hence the latter is not feasible, a contradiction. A similar contradiction can be obtained if it is assumed that p^c is everywhere below p^s. This proves that the p^c and the p^s paths must cross at least once. In order to prove that $T^c < T^s$ it is sufficient to further prove that p^c cuts p^s only once, and from below. Whether p^c cuts p^s in phase I or F

$$(dp^s/dt)/p^s = (r\mu^s + nr\lambda - nU')/p^s$$
$$= (r(\mu^s + n\lambda) - nU')/(\mu^s + \lambda n)$$
$$< r = (dp^c/dt)/p^c$$

Since no intersection can occur at later dates as p^c continues growing at a faster rate than p^s, this completes the proof.

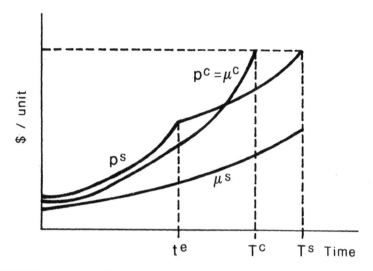

FIGURE 3.3 Competitive, and socially optimal, prices.

optimum and the monitoring costs involved in its implementation, any movement in the right direction can be considered an achievement, and it is a reasonably ambitious objective to aim at accomplishing such improvements in the most efficient way. An abundant economic literature discusses the ways and means of doing so and several practical applications are now in process.

3.4. Transnational pollution in general equilibrium

The fact that the control of pollution is a second-best proposition stresses the need for a general equilibrium analysis. Another complicating factor is the fact that pollution is very often a transnational or transjurisdictional problem. Acid rain across European or the Canada-USA borders, the control of pollution in the Mediterranean Sea, the Rhine River or the St-Laurence Seaway, or the problem of the ozone layer are just some important illustrations of this reality which is also a complicating factor at the regional and municipal levels. Merrifield (1988) analyses alternative policy options, from a positive, and from a welfare, point of view, within a general equilibrium model of bilateral trade with transnational pollution. He uses the North American acid deposition issue as an example. The essence of his analysis, which is static, is the impact of abatement on prices, the movement of goods and productive resources between the countries, and hence their welfare. As key features of the model, pollution is treated as an input D^i to the production function of each sector, $i = 1, 2$, in each country A and B. Although it is productivity enhancing at the sectoral level, pollution has an international social cost because the aggregate transnational pollution which results from individual sources in both countries, $D = D(D^{1A}, D^{2A}, D^{1B}, D^{2B})$, $\partial D/\partial D^{ij} > 0$, determines the efficiency $g(D)$, $g' < 0$, of capital in each sector. Thus the production of sector i in country A is[30]

$$y^{iA} = F^{iA}(g(D)K^{iA}, L^{iA}, E^{iA}, Z^{iA})$$

where Z^{iA}, the regulatory level of pollution abatement equipment, is one of the policy instruments used by each country, independently or in a coordinated manner. A number of interesting real life features are reflected in this formulation. Not only is the transnational pollution level D out of government control because each country regulates its own industries only, but national emission levels are also out of direct government control because the policy instruments which are feasible are also indirect. Indeed, for any regulated level of abatement equipment, firms are free to increase pollution until its marginal product value is zero. Nonetheless the choice of the Z^{iA} by governments affect the equilibrium outcome.

Besides the use of equipment abatement regulation, the author considers the impact of product taxes. He finds that only the former have an unambiguous impact on pollution flows. Because of capital flows between countries, an attempt to reduce pollution by way of a new tax on the output of polluting industries could actually increase pollution. Two other interesting results or reminders are worth stressing. First, a coordinated action, which requires agreement on the choice of an instrument and agreement on the way this instrument is used, is shown to benefit the two countries in differing fashions. In fact, when the use of one instrument unambiguously increases the welfare of one country, there is the possibility of a welfare reduction for the other country. While the author does not discuss the strategic implications of this result, it is clear that they are far-reaching. Such

---

[30] In equilibrium the countries specialize.

a discussion is attempted in Mäller (1989) who finds a similar result in the framework of a parameterized non-cooperative game applied to the European acid rain issue. According to this author, some instruments such as the taxation of emission exports, must be preferred to more efficient ones because they generate enough tax surplus to compensate net losers and are more likely to be implementable on that ground. A second interesting result is that, perhaps unlike conventional trade theory wisdom, the small country is more likely to gain from unilateral action because its abatement efforts, besides reducing domestic pollution, may raise the relative scarcity of the small country products and improve its terms of trade, which attracts a flow of capital from the big country.

4: TRADE AND MACROECONOMIC ISSUES

4.1. Resource models with trade: survival revisited

Trade is frequently invoked as a way to alleviate national technological, or natural resource, constraints. In that tradition, several authors have re-examined the conclusions of the literature on survival, presented in Section 1. While they came up with interesting new theorems, the major contributors to this literature have often either failed to explain why they obtained different results or offered misleading explanations.

Mitra *et al.* (1982) have examined to what extent a small open economy, which depends on an imported resource for production, is under a similar threat of disappearance as the closed, resource-dependent, economy which was studied in Section 1. The basic philosophy is similar to that of Solow (1974b), Stiglitz (1974b) and Dasgupta and Heal (1979) in that trivial cases are ruled out by assumption: the technology is such that survival is impossible without at least some natural resource being used. Mitra *et al.* provide necessary and sufficient conditions on the technology and terms of trade, ensuring survival.

For the particular case of a Cobb-Douglas technology, while Solow had found that survival of the autarkic economy was possible if the elasticity of output with respect to reproducible capital exceeded that with respect to exhaustible resources, Mitra *et al.* establish the possibility of survival even if Solow's condition is violated. They interpret their result as "only a reflection of the familiar 'gains from trade' thesis" (p. 121). This interpretation is inappropriate. Their model of a two-sector economy that trades some of its production against a foreign resource which it needs as an input is not comparable with Solow's one-sector growth model under finite resource constraint. The terms of trade are given exogenously. Changes in the terms of trade affect the easiness with which capital can be substituted for the natural resource in production. If the resource price increases too rapidly relative to the price of exported goods, the open economy is unable to buy enough natural resource, while simultaneously creating enough new capital and maintaining a positive level of consumption. While such easiness of substitution is what is implicitly specified in Solow's share condition, it is unlikely that rising terms of trade are compatible with a constant aggregate share in Mitra *et al.* Indeed, in their model, each of the two sectors has a Cobb-Douglas technology, so that the aggregate technology is not of the Cobb-Douglas type.

So does trade enhance theoretical survival prospects? A closer examination suggests that the answer is negative. The model analysed in Section 1 may be interpreted as a world model. Introduce sub-sectors and countries in such a model: the feasible set can only shrink as more constraints must be satisfied. In particular, impose the condition that the natural-resource-importing part of the world economy must finance its imports by exporting some of its production; then there will be a real drain from the resource-importing part of the world toward the rest of the world. Under such circumstances it is unlikely that its chances of survival will be higher than if it owned some natural resources of its own. This is the essence of Kemp and Long (1984b)'s results. They consider a country with a Cobb-Douglas aggregate technology, while also allowing for non-constant returns to scale. The resource used as a necessary input in production must be acquired under exogenously specified trade terms. This is a major, and well-defined, departure from the world model of Section 1, where the sole constraint in that respect is that imposed by the fact that reserves affect production costs (the Ricardian case) or that reserves are available in finite quantity (the Hotelling case). In fact, in the world model of Section 1, output is divided into consumption and capital accumulation

$$dK/dt = Y - c.$$

In the open economy model of Kemp and Long

$$dK/dt = Y - c - \mu R,$$

where μ is the world price of the natural resource. Clearly, capital accumulation possibilities for the natural-resource-importing part of the world are more restricted in the open economy case. The two models can be made otherwise identical by postulating the same aggregate Cobb-Douglas production function of K and R, which implies a Hotelling world where reserves do not affect production costs, and by postulating that μ rises at the rate of interest, as it should in competitive equilibrium in the Hotelling case[31]. Then it is possible to compare the world model with the open economy model. Not surprisingly, Kemp and Long find that survival is impossible for the open economy, even when the Solow conditions hold, unless there is resource-saving technological change[32].

Our intuition that trade improves an economy's lot is based on comparisons in which trade releases some constraints relative to the no-trade situation, rather than imposing additional constraints. Once it is realized that the literature on survival with trade has imposed additional constraints relative to the literature on survival for the closed economy, its results are no longer ambiguous. All theorems where the trading economy appears to escape the survival conditions spelled out for the world model rely on an implicit release of the resource constraint, usually obtained by postulating a resource price trajectory which is less severe than the exponential path associated with the Hotelling case.

---

[31] In the analysis of Section 1, efficiency was not imposed, so that the time trajectory of μ remained unspecified. However, it is clear that if survival is feasible in general, it is feasible for the efficient solution in particular. While an exponential trajectory for μ is dual to a fixed homogeneous reserve contraint (Hotelling case), there is no simple duality relationship between the price trajectory and the natural resource constraint, including its impact on costs, in general (see equation (1.5) and the ensuing discussion). As a result our comparison between the world, and the open economy, models will be limited to the Hotelling case.

[32] Another survival possibility occurs if the open economy can buy a stock of natural reserves against some of its capital. Once this is done the autarkic option is open; since the latter is formally equivalent to the world model of Section 1, Solow's share condition applies.

4.2. Trade models with natural resources: the basic trade theorems

As is well known, among the four basic trade theorems, two have little to do with trade. They are statements about the structure of production as it relates to endowments (Rybczynski), and the impact of relative output prices on relative input prices (Stolper–Samuelson). The remaining two focus on the effects of trade: what will country A export given its factor endowment and the factor endowment of country B (Heckscher–Ohlin); what impact will trade have on domestic factor prices (Factor price equalization theorems).

This basic theory derives from the 2 × 2 Heckscher–Ohlin model of production. This model is basically static in the sense that production results from the combination of indestructible factors of production[33] within a time invariant technology. One of its major weaknesses is to abstract from the fact that a substantial proportion of world trade involves non-renewable resources and that such resources are important production inputs in most countries. Thanks to several authors, including, overwhelmingly, Kemp and Long (1980b, 1982b, 1984b, 1984d), the basic trade theory has partially been extended to include finite resources as endowments.

Kemp and Long (1984d) consider several alternative ways to introduce non-renewable resources in trade models. None of them involves Ricardian resources; for such non-homogeneous resources there is no trade theory to date. One alternative is the opposite polar case of the standard Heckscher–Ohlin model; Kemp and Long call it the anti-Heckscher–Ohlin model; it could also be called the pure resource trade model. In that model, two homogeneous non-renewable resources (Hotelling resources for short) are substituted for the usual non-produced and indestructible factors of production. However, many of the most interesting trade questions would involve countries endowed with a combination of indestructible factors of production such as capital and labour, and Hotelling resources such as oil. Kemp and Long consider two such models. One is called generalized Heckscher–Ohlin model because it differs from the standard Heckscher–Ohlin model only by the addition of one Hotelling

---

[33] These factors are usually called Ricardian factors in the trade literature, because they are not produced. In order to avoid any confusion with the notion of a Ricardian resource (a non-renewable, non-homogeneous, resource available in unlimited quantity) emphasized throughout this book, they will be called indestructible factors here.

resource to the indestructible factors of production; it is a three-factor model. In the second one, called hybrid, one factor of production is a Hotelling resource while the other factor is of the indestructible type; the hybrid model is a compromise between the Heckscher–Ohlin, and the anti-Heckscher–Ohlin, models.

In the rest of this section, I shall present those resource trade models in a summarized fashion, and sketch the existing results in each case. Obtaining those results was not a trivial endeavour, as it implied recasting traditional formulations in such a way as to allow for the intertemporal dimension imposed by the presence of non-renewable resources on production decisions and the resulting equilibria. The authors also had to reconsider the relevance of such notions as factor endowments, factor intensity, terms of trade, and specialization. They had to innovate in their solution techniques, so that, besides the new trade theorems, their contribution has a methodological interest. I shall try to give a flavour of it while also pointing to the limitations of the endeavour. This is summarized in Table 4.1. Let us start with the anti-Heckscher–Ohlin model.

Anti-Heckscher–Ohlin model
The production of good i is

$$Y^i = f^i(R_1^i, R_2^i), \ i = 1, 2 \tag{4.1}$$

where $f^i(\cdot)$ is assumed to be homogeneous of degree one, strictly quasi-concave and such that each input is essential. R_j^i is the flow of resource j used in sector i. If p is the price of good one relative to the price of good two, i.e. the terms of trade, gross national product is

$$Y = Y^1 + pY^2. \tag{4.2}$$

For any given levels of p and aggregate extraction R_1 and R_2, Y is maximized by optimally allocating R_1 and R_2 between the two sectors,

$$Y = Y(p, R_1, R_2)$$

and the linear homogeneity of the sectoral production functions carries over to the aggregate level so that

$$Y = R_1 Y(p, 1, R_2/R_1) \equiv R_1 y(p, \rho) \tag{4.3}$$

TABLE 4.1

Trade with Resources: Summary of Existing Results

Models / Characteristics	Conventional Heckscher–Ohlin	Anti-Heckscher–Ohlin	Generalized Heckscher–Ohlin	Hybrid
Factor endownments	2 indestructible factors, K and L	2 stocks of Hotelling resources, S_1 and S_2	1 Hotelling resource S; 2 indestructible factors, K and L	1 Hotelling resource S; 1 indestructible factor, K
Technology	For each good, a lin. homog. function of K and L	For each good, a lin. homog. function of the R_1 and R_2 flows	For each good, a lin. homog. function of R, K, L; R separable	For each good, a lin. homog. function of R and K
Concept of factor intensity	Ex.: ind. 1 intensive in K relative to L	Ex.: ind. 1 intensive in R_1 relative to R_2	Ex.: ind. 1 intensive in K relative to L; both ind. have same intens. in R	Ex.: ind. 1 intensive in R relative to K
Trade equilibrium	Static; characterized by terms of trade p	Dynamic; there exists conditions under which p is constant over time	Dynamic; there exists conditions under which p is constant over time	Not characterized or imposed in deriving theorems; p exogenous
Classic theorems 0; S-S; Ry; FPE)*	Yes	Recognizable version exists for the constant p equilibrium	Recognizable version exists for the constant p equilibrium	No theorem under the equilibrium p

*H-O: Heckscher–Ohlin; S-S: Stolper–Samuelson; Ry: Rybcynski; FPE: Factor price equalization.

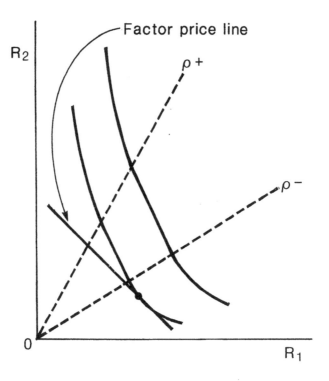

FIGURE 4.1 Isoquants and cone of diversification: anti-Heckscher-Ohlin economy.

where $\rho \equiv R_2/R_1$. One important property of $y(\cdot)$ affects patterns of specialization and trade: when the two industries differ in their factor intensities, for any given p, there exist two values of ρ, $\rho^-(p)$ and $\rho^+(p)$, such that, for $\rho \leq \rho^-(p)$, the economy is specialized in one good, for $\rho \geq \rho^+(p)$, the economy specializes in the other good; in-between both goods are being produced. Thus in Figure 4.1, which represents isoquants for $y(\cdot)$, the economy is diversified inside the cone of diversification delimited by the dashed lines ρ^- and ρ^+.

So far nothing distinguishes the model from a conventional Heckscher–Ohlin trade model. The planning problem for each country, though, is very different from the static problem to be solved in the conventional trade model. Country A, asumed to behave competitively with respect to the rest of the world must jointly solve two extraction problems of a similar nature as the Hotelling problem of Section 1 (country indices are omitted unless otherwise indicated)

$$\text{Max}_{\{R_1, R_2\}} \int_0^\infty e^{-rt} W[Y(p, R_1(t), R_2(t)), p]dt \qquad (4.4)$$

subject to

$$dS_i/dt = -R_i(t); \; R_i(t) \geq 0; \; i = 1, 2$$

$$S_i(t) \geq 0; \; S_i(0) = S_{io} > 0 \text{ given}; \; i = 1, 2$$

where $W(\cdot)$ is an indirect utility function, assumed to be increasing and strictly concave in Y.

Here it is very important to note that p is assumed to be constant. This crucial assumption is in general violated in the two-country equilibrium of a trade model involving non-renewable resources. A terms of trade equilibrium in such a model is in general a trajectory rather than a single number. One of the beauties of Kemp and Long's research programme in this area has been to specify models, and to spell out conditions, under which equilibria with constant terms of trade occur. In such models, the standard Heckscher–Ohlin trade theorems survive, in recognizable form, the substitution of non-renewable factors of production for the indestructible factors of the conventional model. The key ingredients for this result are the type of scarcity – since the shadow prices of a Hotelling resource rise at the interest rate, relative natural resource prices are constant – and the properties of the aggregate production function $Y(\cdot)$ – at constant relative factor prices, when the economy is diversified, the proportion of good 1 relative to good 2 in aggregate production is indeterminate; consequently it can be chosen to be constant. Under the assumption of constant terms of trade, those properties imply, for problem (4.4), the existence of a solution where aggregate output diminishes as factor prices rise according to Hotelling rule, while the composition of output remains constant. If, furthermore, preferences are such that relative marginal utilities are not affected by the level of output, and if those properties are characteristic of both countries, relative output prices (the terms of trade) remain constant in trading equilibrium, validating the initial assumption. The results can be presented in the form of one existence theorem and four (clones of the standard) trade theorems

Theorem 4.1 (existence)
(i) If preferences are strictly convex, homothetic and the same in each of two free-frading countries, and

(ii) if the rate of time preference is everywhere the same and marginal utility is of constant elasticity,

then there exists a trading equilibrium with constant terms of trade.

Theorem 4.2 (Rybczynski)
Let the terms of trade be constant and let both goods be produced along an optimal trajectory; let the same be true after a small increase in $S_i(0)$ there is, at each point of time at which production takes place, an increase in the relative and absolute output of the commodity which is relatively intensive in its use of the ith resource.

Theorem 4.3 (Stolper–Samuelson)
Let the terms of trade be constant and let both goods be produced along an optimal trajectory; let the same be true after a small increase in p_j the price of the jth good. As a result of the increase in p_j there is, at each point of time at which production takes place, an increase in the marginal product (in each industry) of the resource used relatively intensively in the jth industry and a reduction in the marginal product (in each industry) of the other resource.

Theorem 4.4 (Heckscher–Ohlin)
Let there be a trading equilibrium with constant terms of trade and let preferences be strictly convex, homothetic and the same in each country. Then the country which initially is relatively well endowed with the ith Hotelling factor will export the commodity which is relatively intensive in its use of that factor.

Theorem 4.5 (factor price equalization)
If and only if there be a trading equilibrium with both goods being produced along an optimal trajectory in each country, then the marginal product of each resource is the same in both countries.

Remarks
i) The assumption of a constant terms of trade equilibrium is central to most of these results.

ii) In theorem 4.5 the trading equilibrium does not necessarily involve constant terms of trade.

iii) In the constant terms of trade equilibrium the notion of endowment is simplified: the extraction rates in both countries diminish at the same rate, so that the initially better endowed country remains so over the whole programme. Similarly, comparative dynamics are simplified; if production increases at one point in time as a result of an exogenous change in a variable, production will be higher at all dates. Also, the concept of a change in the terms of trade is as trivial as in the static case: the terms of trade cannot improve at one date and worsen at some other time.

Generalized Heckscher–Ohlin model

The anti-Heckscher–Ohlin model is just as extreme as the Heckscher–Ohlin model. The countries in that model do not exhibit the combination of Hotelling endowments and indestructible factor endowments which seems to be the natural ground for interesting new issues to come into focus. The generalized Heckscher–Ohlin model has the necessary ingredient. Unfortunately, as explained below, it is constructed in a way that prevents it from answering any question having to do with differences in industry resource intensities and countries' relative resource endowments.

In each country two final goods can be produced with three internationally immobile factors of production: two conventional, indestructible factors, say K and L, and one Hotelling resource S. K^i (L^i, R^i) represent the portion of K (L, R) used by the ith sector, whose production is

$$Y^i = R_i^a f^i(L^i, K^i) \tag{4.4}$$

where $f^i(\cdot)$ is homogeneous of degree $1 - a$, $0 < a < 1$. Consequently, the technology in each sector is linearly homogeneous in the three factors. What is more important, each sector is equally intensive in its use of the Hotelling resource: since the exponent a is common to both sectors, if $Y^i = Y^j$, $L^i = L^j$ and $K^i = K^j$, then $R^i = R^j$. This assumption is crucial both to the derivation of the trade theorems for this model, and to depriving them of much potential interest.

In fact, from (4.2) and (4.4), gross national product is

$$Y = R^a \lvert (1 + p)(f^1(\cdot) + pf^2(\cdot)) \rvert. \tag{4.5}$$

Since R enters this expression multiplicatively, the maximization of Y by choice of L^i and K^i depends on K, L and p only, and not on R

$$Y = R^a Y^*(p, K, L). \tag{4.6}$$

In both countries, Y is affected by the level of R, which diminishes as the unit rent on S rises exponentially. But this does not affect the allocation of K and L between sectors. As a result, if tastes are identical in each country, and if, in each country, the relative valuations of each good are independent of income, p may remain constant in equilibrium over the whole extraction period. As with the anti-Heckscher–Ohlin model this permits using the highly simplifying constant-terms-of-trade assumption in the formulation of each country's planning problem

$$\underset{\{R\}}{\text{Max}} \int_0^\infty \exp\left(\int_0^t -r(s)ds\right) W\{[R(t)]^a Y^*(p, L, K)\}dt \tag{4.7}$$

subject to

$$dS/dt = -R(t); \; R(t) \geq 0$$

$$S(t) \geq 0; \; S(0) = S_o > 0 \text{ given}$$

where $W(\cdot)$ is an indirect utility function, assumed to be increasing and strictly concave[34].

Theorem 4.6 (existence)[35]

(i) If preferences are strictly convex, homothetic and the same in each of two free-trading countries, and

(ii) if the rate of time preference is everywhere the same and marginal utility is of constant elasticity,

then there exists a trading equilibrium with constant terms of trade.

---

[34] If the country is allowed to borrow and lend at the going interest rate $r(t)$, the intermediate function in (4.7) is $Y(\cdot)$ instead of $W[Y(\cdot)]$; the results are only slightly different.

[35] Slightly weaker conditions apply in the case where the free-trading nations are able to borrow and lend at the given, not necessarily constant, rate of interest.

Theorem 4.7 (Rybczynski)[36]

Let the terms of trade be constant and let both goods be produced along an optimal trajectory; let the same be true after a small increase in L (K). As a result of the increase in L (K) there is, at each point of time at which production takes place, an increase in the relative output of the commodity which is relatively intensive in its use of L (K).

Theorem 4.8 (Stolper–Samuelson)[37]

Let the terms of trade be constant and let both goods be produced along an optimal trajectory; let the same be true after a small increase in p_j, the price of the jth good. As a result of the increase in p_j there is, at each point of time at which production takes place, in each industry, an increase in the ratio of the marginal product of the indestructible factor used relatively intensively in the jth industry over the marginal product of the other indestructible factor.

Theorem 4.9 (Heckscher–Ohlin)

Let there be a trading equilibrium with constant terms of trade. Then the country which initially is relatively well endowed with L (K) will export the commodity which is relatively intensive in its use of L (K).

Theorem 4.10 (factor price equalization)

If, and only if, there is a trading equilibrium and both goods are produced along an optimal trajectory, then the ratios of the marginal products of K and L are the same in both countries.

Remarks

i) Again the equilibrium in theorem 4.10 need not involve constant terms of trade.

ii) The restrictions which ensure the existence of an equilibrium with constant terms of trade, especially the assumption of identical resource intensities in both sectors, restrict the model to conventional predictions

---

[36] Some additional, relatively minor, properties can be established when the countries can borrow and lend at a given rate of interest $r(t)$.

[37] The theorem is slightly reinforced when the countries can borrow and lend at the rate $r(t)$.

on the indestructible factors. Nothing can be said about the pattern of trade between a well resource-endowed country and another country; in particular, if resource processing is a resource intensive activity, none of the above theorems tells us that a well resource-endowed country will export the processed resource in a world where unprocessed resource is an immobile factor!

Hybrid theory
The trade model called hybrid by Kemp and Long is geared toward the questions left unanswered by the generalized Heckscher–Ohlin model. It is a $2 \times 2 \times 2$ model where one factor of production, say K, is indestructible while the other is a Hotelling resource S. Given the rate of extraction R and the terms of trade, maximized gross national product is

$$Y = Y_1 + pY_2$$

$$= Y(p, R, K).$$

This function has the property displayed in Figure 4.1 where K (instead of R_2) must be read on the vertical axis, and R (instead of R_1) must be read on the horizontal axis, while ρ^+ and ρ^- are redefined accordingly and represent upper and lower bounds of capital relative to the extraction rate within which the economy is diversified. Suppose the economy is specialized in the Hotelling-resource intensive industry. If the relative price of R relative to K monotonically increases as a result of the exponential rise in the rent, the switch from that specialization to a specialization in the K intensive industry will occur instantaneously. Suppose the other country was already specialized in the K intensive industry; then only one good would be produced. Suppose the resource intensive product was indispensable; then its price would shoot to infinity as a result of the switch in specialization. More probably, in such a setup, the price of the resource intensive good would start rising before its production was interrupted. One may speculate that, at least over a phase, the equilibrium p would gradually change so as to alter the slope of the linear part of the isoquant in Figure 4.1 in such a way that it coincided with the slope of the factor price line for an extended period. The resource intensive industry could thus stay in production. For these intuitive, but compelling, reasons, it is very unlikely that the terms of trade would remain constant in an equilibrium of this model.

However, this is the assumption under which the theorems are derived, with the caveat that, here, the authors do not provide any sufficient condition under which an equilibrium with constant terms of trade would exist. In view of the foregoing argument, this is hardly surprising. The hybrid theory of international trade is thus incomplete to date. The theorems owed to Kemp and Long depart from the general equilibrium tradition of trade models; they can be viewed only as partial equilibrium properties of two-sector open economies. Furthermore, the prediction of a sudden switch from a resource intensive specialization to a capital intensive specialization is very much a product of the constant terms of trade assumption and is likely to give a highly misleading view of what actually happens in general equilibrium[38]. The extension of trade theory to setups involving Hotelling resources will be complete only when the general equilibrium solution to Kemp and Long's hybrid model is characterized and the corresponding trade theorems are spelled out. Because relative prices and the shares of each sector in gross national product are likely to vary over time in the solution, as well as relative factor endowments, those trade theorems may be far more remote from the classical ones than was the case with the anti-Heckscher–Ohlin and the generalized Heckscher–Ohlin models.

4.3. The Dutch Disease and the Macroeconomy

Introduction
For any individual country, what is the impact on the manufacturing sector of a resource bonanza such as a major discovery or, if the country already is endowed with natural resources, a shift in world demand? What happens to its exchange rate, its unemployment level and its inflation? Among those questions, the first two are central to the pure theory of international trade. As explained in the previous section, however, extensions of that theory to include Hotelling resources did not provide satisfactory answers: the theorems available rule out terms of trade variations and cannot handle situations involving, say, a capital and/or labour intensive manufacturing

---

[38] The authors discuss this issue to some extent (pp. 394–5). In an earlier paper, they have shown that a theorem of Rybczynski type holds when the terms of trade rise exponentially in favour of the resource intensive good.

sector coexisting with another, resource intensive, sector.

This leaves the analyst with the tools of partial equilibrium analysis. One important example of this approach is the partial general equilibrium analysis which has been associated with Dutch Disease economics. Dutch disease is a phenomenon that affects an open macroeconomy after some sudden, exogenous, improvement in its material situation. The name, coined by *The Economist* (1977), is meant to evoke the tough awakening which follows excessive libations. Although normally associated with the adverse effects of resource booms, it has matured to designate most of the evils associated with any favourable, temporary, macro shock: a shrinkage in the manufacturing sector, possibly accompanied by irreversible losses in human capabilities, an appreciation in the real exchange rate, unemployment, inflation, etc . . .

There is an abundant literature on the Dutch Disease; there are also excellent syntheses of that literature. In fact Corden (1984), and Neary and van Wijnbergen (1986a) provide the necessary background and references. The theoretical subsection which follows relies on their contributions heavily; it focuses on real aspects and leaves monetary questions out. The Dutch Disease is also very much a practical problem, so that its analysis is geared toward policy implications; those will be discussed in a special subsection together with some individual country experiences.

Theoretical framework
Most of the well-established theoretical basis underlying the Dutch Disease is static and can be brought to light using the Core Model of Corden and Neary, also adopted by Neary and van Wijnbergen (1986a). A boom is caused by some major technological improvement specific to some sector, or by a windfall discovery of some resource, or still by an exogenous rise in the demand for an exported good. There are three sectors; the booming sector B produces a commodity which is traded on the world market and not locally consumed; the manufacturing sector M produces for both local consumption and for the international market, where its price is exogenously determined; the non-tradeable sector N is oriented toward domestic markets exclusively. The boom has two basic effects on the economy: the spending effect and the factor movement effect[39].

---

[39] This effect is often referred to as the resource movement effect; the resource involved is not the natural resource but some conventional factor of production.

The *spending effect* is the direct income effect of the boom. The additional income injected into the economy raises the demand for both M and N which are assumed to be normal[40]. Since the former is traded on the international market, its price cannot move; the price of N rises, which implies a real exchange rate appreciation.

If there is inter-sector factor mobility this price rise also causes a factor reallocation from sector M to sector N: the manufacturing sector shrinks. This is one form of the *factor movement* effect. This effect may take several other forms which depend on the productive structure of the economy and the specific properties of the factors of production involved. Sector B may use its own internationally hired factors of production; then it it completely isolated from the domestic economy. Alternatively, as will be assumed in the sequel, it may compete with N and M for one or several factors. Capital may be internationally mobile or immobile and, irrespective of this property, it may be sector specific (no competition with other domestic types of capital) or intersectorally mobile. Assume that capital is internationally immobile, sector specific, and fixed in the context of the current static analysis, while labour is internationally immobile but intersectorally mobile. Assume also that labour supply is fixed at L in the aggregate and that demand determines its intersectoral allocation. In obvious notation and remembering that output prices in B and M are exogenously given

$$L_M + L_B + L_N =$$
$$L^M(w) + L^B(w) + L^N(w/q) = L \qquad (4.8)$$

where w is the real wage, expressed in terms of M, while q is the real price of N, also in terms of M. (4.8) defines the labour market equilibrium line LL in Figure 4.2.

The sole product market which must clear domestically is the market for N. Since B is not consumed domestically and since the price for M is given, the demand for N is a function of q and real income y. Equilibrium on the N market must satisfy

$$S(q/w) = D(q, y)$$

which defines the NN locus in Figure 4.2.

---

[40] M, N, and B will be used to designate the goods, as well as the sectors, alternatively.

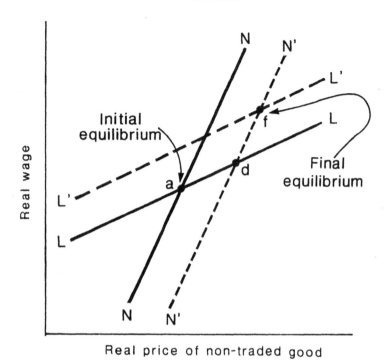

FIGURE 4.2 Spending and factor-movement effects of a boom.

The factor movement effect has several components. First, the boom directly raises $L^B(\cdot)$, shifting the LL locus up. The additional demand is met by labour movements away from N and M. Second, since the spending effect, shifting NN to the right, has raised q, labour demand has increased (without shifting) in that sector. The net effect is ambiguous in N. On the contrary, in M, there is no change in labour demand; M loses workers to both B and N. So the final equilibrium, besides higher w and q, involves a labour reallocation away from M, toward B and, possibly, toward N. The rise in q (a real exchange rate appreciation) and the shrinking of the manufacturing sector, are the agreed-upon symptoms of the Dutch Disease[41].

---

[41] The exogenous rise in y has often been labelled inflationary and the rise in q and w assimilated to inflation; of course they are just a once-and-for-all shock, and once-and-for-all relative price adjustments in this static model of the real side of the economy.

Before turning to more controversial symptoms, a few remarks are appropriate. First, the fact that the existing traded good sector has been labelled M should not obscure the fact that it may just as well be an open agricultural sector. The so-called deindustrialization effect is in fact a reduction in the size of the existing world trading sector, whatever its activity. Indeed, in several developing countries, the sectors which suffered from a resource boom were agricultural sectors. Second, the scenario just described must only be viewed as a consensus approximation of the real effects of a resource boom. Other equilibrium models may yield quite different outcomes; those are considered unlikely. For example, nobody seriously questions the assumption that all goods are normal in the analysis. Similarly, the 'paradox' model of Corden and Neary (Corden, 1984) is not considered empirically relevant. In that model, the factors are still assumed internationally immobile, but the assumption of intersectoral capital immobility is relaxed; capital can move freely between M and N, while labour can move between M, N, and B. Taken in isolation from the B sector, M and N constitute a Heckscher–Ohlin economy, whose endowment in labour is reduced when the factor movement effect has labour move toward the B sector. By Rybczynski theorem, this reduces the output of the labour intensive sector and raises, at least in relative terms, the output of the capital intensive sector. If M is the capital intensive sector, the Rybczynski effect may cause an expansion of M, which may offset the spending effect and reverse the conventional deindustrialization prediction.

Deindustrialization and real exchange rate appreciation remain also the likely outcomes when the assumption of international capital immobility is relaxed, with capital remaining sector specific. In the plausible case where, in each sector, capital rents move in the same direction as output when capital is immobile, international mobility will cause international capital flows toward the sectors where rents have increased –B and, possibly, N– and away from M. This will moderate the price and rent effects of the boom while adding to the quantity adjustments. Deindustrialization will be more pronounced. In the extreme case of perfect international capital mobility and constant returns to scale in all sectors, the M sector can be in production only if its input prices are identical to those in the rest of the world. Since the spending effect of the boom raises w, effectively allowing B to pay workers a rent over and above world wage,

M disappears entirely while *q* adjusts so as to ensure zero profits.

The nature of the shock is not always irrelevant as assumed so far. While maintaining the assumption that *B* is not domestically consumed, consider the difference between a boom caused by a local discovery, at given world demand conditions, and a boom caused by a shift in world demand given existing reserves. In the former instance the relative price of *B* is unchanged while in the latter it is increased, as well as the rent on the resource in the ground. Suppose that *B* involves some processing which may be carried out at the point of origin (domestically) or at the point of destination (abroad), with transportation costs per dollar unit being lower for the processed than for the unprocessed commodity. If capital is more expensive domestically than in the rest of the world, it is easy to construct examples where domestic processing is optimal before a rise in the resource rent while, after the boom, processing is more profitable abroad. In that case, besides the usual spending and factor movement effects, a price shock will cause processing to migrate abroad, while a discovery will cause the domestic processing industry to expand[42].

The full-employment equilibrium framework used so far has not permitted the question of unemployment to be raised. Taking account of the spillovers between markets arising from wage and price rigidities, Figure 4.2 can be partitioned à la Malinvaud (1977) into a region of classical unemployment *C*, a region of Keynesian unemployment *K*, and a region of repressed inflation R[43]. The boom shifts the equilibrium and the region limits in the way indicated in Figure 4.3. The new equilibrium, identical to point *d* in Figure 4.2, is drawn on the assumption that there is no factor movement effect, implying that sector *B* is completely isolated from *M* and *N*. Price and wage rigidities

---

[42] For example, suppose that the cost of making one unit of the processed resource available on the world market is

$$C_D = \mu^{1/2} V_D^{1/2} + T_p \qquad \text{with domestic processing and}$$
$$C_W = \mu^{1/2} V_W^{1/2} + T_r \qquad \text{with processing abroad}$$

where μ is the resource rental, V_D (V_W) is the domestic (foreign) rental price of capital, and T_p (T_r) is the unit transportation cost of the processed (raw) commodity. With $V_D = 4$; $V_W = 1$; $T_p = 1$; $T_r = 3$, one can check that domestic processing is preferable when $\mu = 1$ while processing abroad is preferable when $\mu = 4$.

[43] For a more detailed exposition, see Neary and Wijnbergen (1986b, pp. 19–23); for a complete textbook treatment with a numerical example, see Campan and Grimaud (1988).

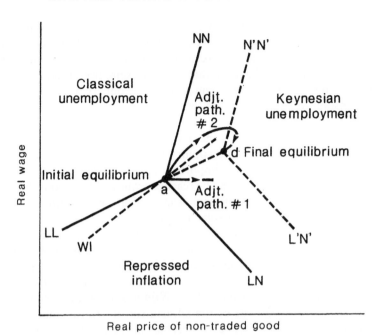

FIGURE 4.3 Effects of a boom with wage and price rigidities (no factor-movement effect).

prevent any instantaneous adjustment from a to d. The question becomes: assuming the economy will eventually reach the new equilibrium d, what situations will emerge during the transition, i.e. which regions will the path between a and d cross? a is the initial point on that path. Not surprisingly, since the initial shock amounts to a Keynesian income stimulus which would be administered in a full employment situation, it moves the region of Keynesian unemployment away from the initial equilibrium, leaving it at the limit between regions C and R: right after the shock, the labour market is in equilibrium but there is excess demand for N which calls, somehow, for a rise in q. What will happen to w while q rises? If w stays constant, as in path 1, the economy enters a phase of repressed inflation, involving both excess demand for L and for N. If, on the contrary, the increase in q is foreseen and taken into account in wage settlements, an adjustment path such as 2 may occur, causing the emergence of classical unemployment combined with excess demand for N. Whether one or the other is more likely to occur crucially depends on economic institutions, in particular the prevalent type of wage indexation. Van Wijnbergen (1984b) assumes that real consumption wage can be reduced only by temporary unemployment. If only N was consumed, the constant real consumption wage would be on a straight line through the origin and a; if only M was consumed it would be on an horizontal line through a. In general the consumption wage is constant along a line such as WI. For a country like Saudi Arabia where much of the consumption basket is imported, WI is almost horizontal, and likely to lie below point d. d can be reached from a without going below WI (reducing the consumption wage). For such countries the adjustment is less likely to involve unemployment. For countries such as Mexico and Venezuela where a substantial part of the consumption is local, non-traded, production, the WI curve is probably above d and the adjustment to a lower consumption wage at d must involve a period of unemployment; an adjustment path such as 2 is perhaps to be expected. According to Neary and van Wijnbergen these results accord well with the stylized facts of the adjustment of several countries to natural resource discoveries and increases in the prices of resources.

Wage and price rigidities often coexist with factor rigidities, such as the reluctance of labour to move to another sector. If the labour force in the M sector cannot be reduced as much as required by the new equilibrium, unemployment can be avoided in that sector only if its wage is set lower than in the B and N sectors. Attempts to maintain wage parity with other sectors will cause unemployment in M.

Policy implications and individual country experiences

The symptoms of the Dutch Disease are basically negative aspects of a good event. Does the Dutch Disease call for a cure? Clearly such a cure should not jeopardize the underlying benefits. Preventing the economy from adjusting to its new equilibrium in order to keep M from shrinking would also prevent society from reaping some of the benefits of the boom. Intervention, even temporary, may be damaging. For example, despite the negative connotation of the term, overshooting of the exchange rate during the adjustment period, which Neary and Purvis (1983) have shown may occur, is not a bad thing in itself; preventing such overshooting may involve a slower adjustment and a postponement of the period when maximum benefits can be realized.

The arguments in favour of a cure to the Dutch Disease are the usual arguments in favour of government intervention: correction of market imperfections and externalities on efficiency grounds, and for distributional purposes. Protection of the M sector by tariffs or exchange rate policy on distributional grounds should be avoided, as the same aim can be achieved in a less distortive fashion by taxing B and subsidizing the workers in M and/or compensating those who move. The case for specific government intervention on efficiency grounds is weak: if imperfections are present, they are likely to be present whether or not the economy enjoys a resource boom; existing corrective features may have to be adjusted, but this does not call for new measures. However, some externalities, which are latent in the economy but do not require intervention in normal circumstances, may have to be corrected during the adjustment period.

A version of the infant industry argument is sometimes invoked when it is expected that the M sector will have to recover once the boom is over. Its decline during the boom, it is argued, may involve irreversible physical and human capital losses which will preclude a later recovery. This argument requires some externality in order to be valid. Lack of information and foresight, and, especially, imperfect capital markets, may affect private decisions among small firms, especially in developing countries. In all countries, the learning-by-doing argument, which claims that technology is to some extent a public good that firms can assimilate only progressively by practicing their trade, may also justify intervention.

Whether explicitly on those grounds or for other reasons, governments have been deeply involved in the management of resource booms. This is true of very diverse countries and is documented in an abundant literature (see several of the contributions in Neary and van Wijnbergen, 1986b, and for a focus on developing countries, many of the references in Decaluwé and Martens, 1988). Most resource rich countries seem to have experienced the major symptoms of Dutch Disease, and to have adopted a mixture of purely macroeconomic policies (monetary and exchange rate policies), together with policies concerning the use of the resource bonanza. The following paragraphs are devoted to the latter type only. It is appropriate to distinguish between developed countries, poor developing countries, and capital-surplus developing countries.

In the last, population was small relative to the magnitude of the boom. The prospect of running out of resource was considered remote enough to preclude a transitory adjustment to a temporary period of prosperity; a permanent adjustment to a higher growth trajectory was requested. In most instances governments considered two basic options: investment in the local economy and investment in the rest of the world. Since the local economy was close to non-existent, the first option often took the form of mega-projects, while the non-traded sector also grew substantially. Both requested substantial imports of labour. In that respect, the experience of capital surplus countries was different from the standard model (*The Economist*, 1988). The conditions under which such projects were carried were not otherwise very different in capital surplus countries, than in developing countries. If one can judge from the evidence on big projects in such countries (Gelb, 1986), foreign and portfolio investment is likely to have been a better way to carry wealth into the future than direct domestic investment. While investments in local projects often failed to pass standard viability criteria, their justification may have run along standard infant industry and learning-by-doing arguments. It must be noted here that, since they enjoyed a capital surplus, these countries, unlike other developing countries, did not face imperfect capital markets.

The experience of developed countries broadly appears to conform with the theoretical model. In those countries, however, it is often difficult to separate out the impact of the resource boom from other influences. In particular the depressing effect of higher energy prices on the world economy may have affected the traded sectors in those countries as much as the Dutch Disease. Also, the decline in the share of manufacturing and the growth in the share of the service sector, which characterize mature economies, may mistakenly be interpreted as a symptom of Dutch Disease. Resource rents varied in magnitude, high on oil and gas during the Opec golden area, lower on other resources, but a substantial part accrued to the public sector (see Forsyth, 1986, on Great Britain and Australia; Kremers, 1986, on the Netherlands; Helliwell, 1981, on Canada). Nevertheless, most authors find that resource rents have been spent mostly on consumption. This is true of those rents which did accrue to the public sector as taxes and levies. This is also true of the substantial part which was distributed directly in the form of higher wages or lower energy prices. Of course some public investments resulted from resource rents; those are difficult to evaluate, though, because resource revenues were not earmarked for particular purposes, with such exceptions as some energy infrastructure investments which were financed out of oil revenues, and investments into the Alberta Heritage Savings Trust Fund.

In developing countries, a high proportion, about four-fifths, of the windfalls were also received by governments. They used them with three central objectives: growth of the non-oil economy, the extension of national control, and reduced oil dependance (Gelb, 1986). About half of the windfall was invested into the local economy, with a disappointing impact on growth. On average, the non-oil economies of Algeria, Ecuador, Indonesia, Nigeria, Trinidad and Tobago, and Venezuela, were 4.1 per cent smaller during 1979–81 than they would have been had they maintained their 1967–72 growth trajectories (p. 78). Even correcting for specific country circumstances that might have explained a slowdown in growth, actual performance for 1972–81 appears to have fallen well short of potential, a likely sign of Dutch Disease. It must be pointed out that several investments, notably in transportation and education, with their long gestation lags, may not have produced much of their return over Gelb's study period. However, even if this could be adjusted for, it is clear that the yield on domestic investment has fallen well short of that available abroad. While they have increased the sphere of domestic control, governments have not succeeded in reducing the dependance on oil and gas exports as a source of foreign revenues. Indonesia appears to have been the most successful in strenthening its agriculture and industry. One apparent explanation for this relative success is less reliance on big capital intensive industrial projects. As Warr (1986) points out, Indonesia was also to a certain extent lucky, for internal political reasons, to abstain from borrowing heavily on international markets in the late 1970s, thus avoiding the debt crisis which was to plague many other LDCs in the 1980s.

4.4 Other issues

Many other fascinating issues have been raised in the area of international relations involving natural resources. It is impossible to do justice here to the imagination and cleverness of the authors who have tried to throw some light on those issues. The interested reader is invited to refer to the original papers.

Given the relative inability of extended standard trade theory to deal with natural resources, some authors have used computable international general equilibrium models to address certain questions. Chichilnisky (1986) constructs a two-region model of the world, with an industrial North producing consumption and industrial goods using labour capital and oil, and a monopolistic oil exporting South purchasing some of those goods. What the author shows is that, depending on the technology and the initial level of prices, a rise in the price of oil may benefit both the North and the South in general equilibrium. This points to the possibility of international cooperation. However, configurations exist where the interests of both regions diverge, as is more frequently assumed within the North-South debate. Chichilniski *et al.* (1986) use a similar approach but focus on international indebtness. In their North-South model, the trade surplus of the South is used to finance the development of the oil sector, so that there is an explicit link between the financial and the production sectors. The paper studies the impact of changes in the values of the debt on both the borrowing and lending regions. Who benefits and who loses from the accumulation of debt? Is cooperation a possibility or do the regions necessarily have conflicting interests? A loan may have a beneficial effect on the equilibrium of the lending country, because it leads to more abundant oil exports and lower oil prices. This externality may in some circumstances justify the compensation of private banks for extending privately unprofitable loans to the South, or to help them reschedule debts.

The same issue is examined from a different point of view in the literature on the recycling of oil revenues. Raucher (1987), Hillman and Long (1985), and Hoel (1981), among others, consider alternative forms of the joint capital-investment/extraction decisions of countries with influence on the rate of return on non-resource assets. In all cases the optimal extraction rate is affected by the necessity to take account of its impact on the capital market. In some circumstances, it may be optimal for an oil exporting monopoly to subsidize oil importers' borrowing.

The influence of resource producers on financial markets has also recently been examined under a new light by Phlips and Harstad (1988). In their paper, two duopolists extract their given reserves while having access to a futures market for their output, whose demand is stochastic. The problem is formulated as a two-stage game; the existence of futures markets is found to be profit enhancing and profitable speculation transforms the temporal evolution of extraction rates and the spot price.

The desirability to process non-renewable resource exports domestically is a constant scheme in the development literature. Although more sporadically, it has also been addressed in the resource literature, which is reviewed by Kumar (1988). Kumar introduces his own, versatile and pedagogical, framework. Three major elements play a crucial role in the results.

If the first element, the necessity to acquire processing capital services on the international market under balance of payment constraint, is the sole consideration, the bang-bang solution to the planning problem of the country involves a final phase of domestic processing, which may or may not follow a finite period over which the economy is diversified and a finite period over which no processing takes place. This works as follows. As the resource rent rises exponentially, processing, possibly as a hypothetical alternative, uses the ore more and more parsimoniously; as a result, the marginal product of one unit of ore in processing rises and, at some stage, its value overtakes the (constant) marginal product value of ore in the form of unprocessed exports. At this point, domestic processing starts. This result relies on the absence of a general equilibrium mechanism whereby the absolute and relative prices of both the unprocessed resource and the processed resource would rise over time to reflect increased ore scarcity.

The second element is transportation costs; if they are lower for the processed resource than for the bulkier, unprocessed, resource, the opposite result, illustrated in footnote 42, is likely to arise. At low resource rent, processing may be highly resource intensive and justify domestic processing to save on transportation costs. As the rent rises over time, processing becomes more intensive in other factors, so that the transportation cost advantage of domestic processing is reduced, and the whole activity may be displaced.

The third element is market power. Kumar shows that domestic processing may be optimal for a resource monopoly while foreign processing would be adequate if the same resource was exploited competitively. This result is obtained in the absence of transportation cost differences.

5. TAXATION

5.1. Introduction

Taxation is a very important aspect of non-renewable resource exploitation. The *in situ* resource being most often under public ownership,
the tax system is used as a device by which the public collects the rent
owed to it by the user of the resource. This role is unique to resource
taxation, although it is played with instruments that are not necessarily
particular to extractive sectors. In fact the major instruments of
resource taxation are the royalty, the severance tax, various leases for
the right to explore or exploit, but also the rate of return tax, import
and export tariffs, and, not least of all, the corporate income tax,
usually with special provisions.

Besides rent appropriation, the taxing institutions are naturally
concerned with efficiency. Resource taxes usually alter taxpayer behaviour. While this is true in any economic activity, the particular effects
to be considered are often unusual and highly specific in resource
industries. Firms may alter their plans with respect to rates of extraction, cut-off grades, and mine or oil-field lives, as well as their choice
of inputs and their exploration activities[44]. As they occur in economies
which are likely to be subject to various other distortions, those effects
should ideally be analysed in a second-best framework.

Resource tax revenues are merged with other tax incomes; they are
used to serve the same purposes as regular taxes, such as income
redistribution and stabilization. However their share of general tax
revenues is in some instances so high that the authorities are led to
design their resource taxes with those purposes in mind. For example,
during the 1970s, Canadian oil taxes were discussed in redistributive
terms (Heaps and Helliwell, 1985) as well as rent collecting devices;
similarly, the proceeds of North Sea oil and gas were considered an
important macroeconomic matter.

To complicate matters, the taxing authorities are subject to various
constraints which may lead them to behave strategically: import tariffs
on resource products may be set so as to extract a rent which would

---

[44]For good introductions to resource tax systems and taxation issues see Harberger
(1955), Conrad and Hool (1980), Heaps and Helliwell (1985), and, for a more theoretical
approach, Dasgupta, Heal, and Stiglitz (1980).

otherwise be collected by the exporting country; resource extracting regions may be under different jurisdictions which compete for activity and revenues.

Obviously, the field is rich in fascinating issues, some of which are almost untouched, some others more thoroughly explored. In the next subsections, I shall deal with the distortive effects of various taxes, first in a simple Hotelling world, then in a simple Ricardian world, and, finally, in more complex situations involving capital decisions, exploration, and stochastic events. I will also briefly go over second-best situations and general equilibrium, risk sharing, and strategic behaviour on the part of the taxing authorities.

5.2. Resource taxation in a simple Hotelling world

The simple Hotelling world of this subsection is a particular case of the model described in 1.2. The firm extracts a homogeneous resource from a given initial stock of reserves S_0. Its extraction cost $C(R)$ is independent of S, and the fact that input prices do not appear in $C(\cdot)$ implies that those prices are assumed constant over time. In reality some taxes, such as the corporate income tax, affect factor prices so that the after-tax cost function is different from the before-tax cost function. For this reason, the corporate income tax will be given a separate treatment; at this stage all taxes are of a kind which does not affect the input mix. It is also assumed that the firm does not incur any particular cost and does not realize any particular benefit at closure time T, whether tax induced or of a technological nature. In particular, all inputs are leased and perfectly malleable, so that the firm has no residual value at T. Finally, aggregation issues are avoided by making the assumption that all firms are identical; this rules out entry and exit, a possibility discussed in Burness (1976), to whom we owe much of the analysis presented now and whose methodology has set the standards for this vein of literature.

The effect of alternative taxes will be described by comparing the extraction programmes of a firm or industry under taxation, and without tax. The no-tax solution, which is also the social optimum under competition, will be denoted by attaching the superscript '*' to the relevant variables; thus, for example, T^* and $S^*(t)$, respectively, denote the optimal terminal date, and the stock of remaining reserves at t, in a no-tax situation. T and $S(t)$ now refer to tax situations and, as before, it will be made clear whether they should be understood as optimized or not. Unless otherwise mentioned the focus is on the competitive case, so that, in the tradition of partial analysis, any departure from the '*' solution can be interpreted as a distortion away from the first-best situation.

The competitive firm selects an extraction path $R(\cdot)$ and a closure date T is such a way as to solve

$$Maximize \int_0^T e^{-rt}[p(t)R(t) - C(R(t)) - Z(S(t), R(t), p(t), t)]dt$$

subject to

(5.1)

$$-dS/dt = R(t) \geq 0, \text{ with } S(0) = S_0 \text{ given}$$ (5.2)

where $Z(S, R, p, t)$, the tax function, takes up various specific forms depending on the tax under study. As before, it is assumed that p does not rise at more than the discount rate and is high enough at all dates to cover extraction costs and the tax. $C(\cdot) + Z(\cdot)$ is jointly convex in (S, R) for $\underline{R} \geq R \geq 0$, where $\underline{R}$ is the extraction rate at which average cost-plus-tax is minimum.

As a first approximation, an oil company or a mine may be subject to the following taxes during its extraction phase[45]:

$Z(\cdot) = f(t)$: franchise tax or license fee or fixed property tax;
$Z(\cdot) = s(t)R(t)$: severance tax or royalty;
$Z(\cdot) = s(t)p(t)R(t)$: ad valorem severance tax or royalty;
$Z(\cdot) = g(t)S(t)$: ad valorem property tax[46];
$Z(\cdot) = u(\cdot)[p(t)R(t) - C(R)]$: profit, rate of return, or
    resource rent tax.

The Hamiltonian for problem (5.1) is (omitting time arguments)

$$H(\cdot) = e^{-rt}[(p - \mu)R - C(R) - Z(S, R, p, t)].$$ (5.3)

---

[45]The corporate income tax is treated in a separate section.

[46]Property taxes are often defined according to land area; then, since this is invariant as S gets depleted, the franchise tax is a good representation, especially if $f(t)$ is periodically adjusted to reflect changes in land value. In a resource extraction context, the property derives its value from its reserve content; the property tax should be based on the value of remaining reserves. While there are several ways to evaluate the value of $S(t)$, an important special case is $g(t)S(t) = ge^{rt}S(t)$ which applies a fixed rate to the true value of remaining reserves.

By the maximum principle

$$p = \mu + dC/dR + \partial Z/\partial R. \qquad (5.4)$$

This condition differs from the no-tax case not only because of the tax term, but because μ is likely to differ from μ^*. Although the discount rate is unaffected by the tax under the current assumptions, Hotelling rule may take a different form than in the no-tax case because of the possibility that the tax depends on remaining reserves

$$d\mu/dt = r\mu + \partial Z/\partial S. \qquad (5.5)$$

At T, the Hamiltonian must vanish. If T is finite, this implies

$$p = \mu + C(\cdot)/R - Z(\cdot)/R.$$

Combining this with (5.4) one has at T

$$dC/dR + \partial Z/\partial R = C(\cdot)/R + Z(\cdot)/R. \qquad (5.6)$$

In order to focus on industry effects, and keeping in mind the aggregation issues already mentioned, assume that (5.4)–(5.6) are sectoral relationships and that sector demand is $p(t) = P(R(t))$, with $P(\cdot)$ decreasing in R[47]. In the perfect information equilibrium price must equalize the supply and demand of R, a condition which is imposed by substituting $P(\cdot)$ for $p(t)$ in (5.4). Totally differentiating the resulting expression with respect to t, and eliminating μ and $d\mu/dt$ using (5.4) and (5.5), one has

$$(dR/dt)[dP/dR - d^2C/dR^2 - \partial^2Z/\partial R^2 - (\partial^2Z/\partial R\partial p)(dP/dR)]$$
$$= r[p - dC/dR - \partial Z/\partial R] + \partial Z/\partial S + \partial^2Z/\partial R\partial t$$
$$- (\partial^2Z/\partial R\partial S)R. \qquad (5.7)$$

Together with the terminal condition (5.6), this differential equation defines the optimal extraction path $R(\cdot)$ implicitly. In particular, in the absence of a tax, it reduces to

$$(dR^*/dt)[dP/dR - d^2C/dR^2] = r[p - dC/dR] \qquad (5.7^*)$$

which is a particular case of (1.6) and is immediately seen to imply that R^* decreases over time.

---

[47] It is easily verified that this meets the earlier assumption on the rate of growth of $p(t)$.

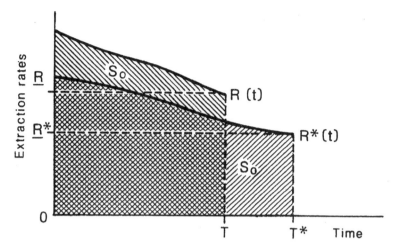

FIGURE 5.1 Hotelling model: effect of a franchise tax.

It is now possible to analyze the effect of alternative taxes on the optimum extraction path, on its duration, and on the rent. In order to do this Burness (1976) used a technique which lends itself to a graphical analysis in (R, t) space.

Figure 5.1 depicts the case of a *franchise tax* $(Z (\cdot) = f(t))$. Since the same stock S_0 is extracted with, and without, a tax, the areas under the curves $R(t)$ and $R^*(t)$ must be identical, so that the reserve constraint (5.2) can be readily checked on the diagram. Furthermore, by (5.6), marginal cost exceeds average cost at T while, in the no-tax case, (5.6) requires marginal cost to be equal to average cost at T^*. It follows that $R(T)$ exceeds $R^*(T^*)$ as depicted. Finally (5.7) reduces to (5.7*). This means that if, at some date t, extraction rates were identical with and without a tax, then $R(t)$ and $R^*(t)$ would have the same slope; but then $R(t + \epsilon) = R^*(t + \epsilon)$ and, as a result, the slopes are also identical at $t + \epsilon$. Repeating this argument, it follows that, if $R(t) = R^*(t)$ at some t, then $R(t) = R^*(t)$ at all dates. Since at closure time $R(T) > R^*(T^*)$ and the curves are downward sloping, this requires $T < T^*$. However two curves which differ only in that one, $R(t)$, covers a shorter period than the other one, $R^*(t)$, cannot generate identical areas. This violation of the reserve constraint implies that there does not exist any date t at which

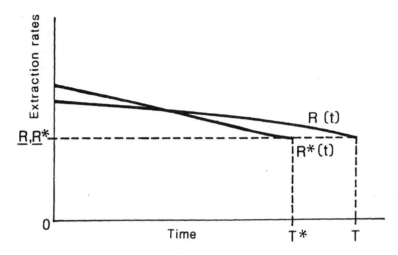

FIGURE 5.2 Hotelling model: effect of a constant severance or royalty.

$R(t) = R^*(t)$. This leaves only two possibilities: either $R(t)$ is everywhere above $R^*(t)$, or the opposite. It is immediate to check that, with $\underline{R} > \underline{R}^*$, the areas under the curve can be identical only in the former case, as depicted in Figure 5.1. The franchise tax thus causes existing reserves to be depleted faster than in the absence of tax. The intuitive explanation is that this shortening of the extraction period allows the firms to pay a lower cumulative tax bill than if they did not adjust their extraction trajectory.

Now consider a *severance tax or royalty*. The same approach is followed as with the franchise tax. By (5.6), $R(T) = R^*(T^*)$. (5.7) reduces to

$$(dR/dt)[dP/dR - d^2C/dR^2] = r[p - dC/dR - s(t)] + ds/dt.$$
$$(5.7s)$$

Assume that the tax rate is constant $(ds/dt = 0)$; if at some date $t\,R(t) = R^*(t)$, then $dR/dt > dR^*/dt$. In other words, if the R and R^* paths cross each other, R must cut R^* from below; furthermore, this can happen only once. It is also easily seen that both paths cannot meet the area-under-the-curve condition while terminating at identical extraction rates $R^*(T^*) = R(T)$, unless they do cross each other and the steeper one spans a shorter period. The solution must be as depicted in Figure 5.2.

At any given initial reserve level ($t = 0$), imposing a constant severance tax causes R to be reduced relative to the no-tax case; furthermore, the extraction period is lengthened. Unlike the franchise, the firm cannot avoid the tax by shortening the extraction period. Instead, the tax has the effect of an increase in marginal cost, whose static output reducing effect carries out to the dynamic context of resource extraction; however, since the tax cannot affect total cumulative extraction in the Hotelling model, the reduced extraction rate translates into a longer extraction period. When the tax rate is not constant, anything can happen. In particular, it is possible to select $s(t)$ in such a way that $rs(t) = ds/dt$ at all dates; in that case, (5.7) reduces to (5.7*) and the tax does not affect the extraction path. What is the yield of such a neutral tax? It is easily determined. The transversality condition (5.6) reduces to

$$P(R) = \mu + C(R)/R + s. \qquad (5.6s)$$

This compares with the tax free case

$$P(R^*) = \mu^* + C(R^*)/R^*. \qquad (5.6^*)$$

Since $R^* = R$, it follows that $\mu + s = \mu^*$ at $T = T^*$. Also, since both s and μ grow at the rate r, they represent the same proportion of each other and of μ^* at all dates. Thus this particular severance tax is collecting a constant proportion of the tax-free rent, which is also the before-tax rent. It is in fact equivalent to a rent tax, which also leaves the extraction path unaffected, as shown further below.

The *ad valorem severance tax or royalty* turn out to have identical properties as their output based counterparts. Let us now investigate the effect of a *property tax based on the value of the resource property*. Since $Z(S, R, p, t) = g(t)S(t)$, (5.7) reduces to

$$(dR/dt)\left[dP/dR - \partial^2 C/\partial R^2\right] = r\left[p - \partial C/\partial R\right] + g(t). \qquad (5.7g)$$

As a result, if the tax-free and the property tax extraction rates cross each other, $dR/dt < dR^*/dt$. Since (5.6) requires $R(T) = R^*(T^*)$ for this tax, the extraction paths indeed must cross if the surfaces they generate are also to be identical. The sole possible configuration is depicted in Figure 5.3. It requires a faster extraction than in the tax-free situation, which is selected by the firm as a way to shorten the period over which

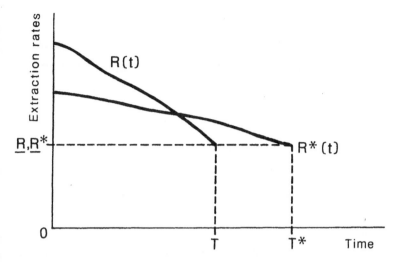

FIGURE 5.3 Hotelling model: effect of a property tax based on the value of the resource property.

it is liable to pay the property tax; this result applies whether or not the resource unit is properly evaluated.

A *pure profit tax*, such as the rate-of-return tax was advocated by Garnaut and Ross (1975, 1979) and further discussed by, among others, Heaps and Helliwell (1985), and Heaps (1985). Naturally, being based on pure profits, the interest for this type of taxation has arisen from its potential neutrality. As shown now, if a neutral tax is defined as a tax which leaves the competitive extraction path unchanged, the rate of return tax is not neutral in the progressive rate versions which have usually been implemented. With $Z(\cdot) = u(\pi)\pi$, $\pi = pR - C(R)$ being pure profits, (5.7) reduces to

$$(dR/dt)\{(dP/dR - d^2C/dR^2)[1 - (u + \pi du/d\pi)] \qquad (5.7\pi)$$
$$- (2du/d\pi + \pi d^2u/d\pi^2)(p - dC/dR)[(p - dC/dR)$$
$$+ RdP/dR]\} = r[(p - dC/dR)[1 - (u + \pi du/d\pi)]$$

or after some manipulations

$$dR/dt = (dR*/dt)[(dP/dR - d^2C/dR^2)[1 - (u + \pi du/d\pi)]$$

$$/\{(dP/dR - d^2C/dR^2)[1 - (u + \pi du/d\pi)] - (2du/d\pi$$

$$+ \pi d^2u/d\pi^2)(p - dC/dR)[(p - dC/dR) + RdP/dR]\}].$$

Since (5.6) requires $R(T) = R*(T*)$, the tax is neutral if and only if (5.7π) reduces to (5.7*). It can be verified that this is the case if and only if the tax rate $u(\pi)$ is chosen in such a way that

$$2du/d\pi + \pi d^2u/d\pi^2 = 0 \text{ for all } \pi^{[48]}. \tag{5.8}$$

Besides the flat rate tax, this condition is satisfied by

$$u(\pi) = A - B\pi^{-1}, 0 < A \le 1, B > 0.$$

It can be seen that this gives a progressive tax, with $u(\cdot)$ rising in π and tending toward A as π tends to ∞. However, for low values of π, $u(\pi)$ is negative. In fact Z is simply a negative profit tax $u(\pi)\pi = -B + A\pi$.

Tax authorities can implement a progressive rate of return taxes while preserving neutrality only if they accept to subsidize low profits. In cyclical industries such as resource extraction, this implies sharing a higher proportion of the risk than under a flat-rate tax. Governments have avoided this route and, instead, those progressive rate of return taxes that have been implemented are distortive. However their exact effect depends on the elasticity of demand and the value of the resource. A tax whose yield is positive, rising, and convex, in π must satisfy $u + \pi du/d\pi < 0$ and $2u + \pi d^2u/d\pi^2 \ge 0$. It can be shown that such a tax slows down the extraction of highly valuable Hotelling resources (μ high) whose demand elasticity is relatively high (dP/dR small) and, conversely, speeds up the extraction of widely available Hotelling resources (μ small) whose demand elasticity is high (dP/dR high in absolute value).

5.3 Resource taxation in a simple Ricardian world

It will be remembered that, in a Ricardian model of resource extraction, ultimate cumulative extraction depends on economic conditions. This happens because geological conditions are not homogeneous, so that extraction costs vary as extraction proceeds. Closure occurs when price

---

[48]If we write the tax as $G(\pi(R,p)) \equiv Z(R,p)$, it can be seen that (5.8) is in fact $d^2G/d\pi^2 = 0$, meaning that the tax is linear in π.

no longer covers marginal extraction cost and this condition determines the amount of reserves left in the ground and deemed uneconomical. Obviously, taxation may affect it. Analysis is harder than in the Hotelling case because one has to identify both effects on the extraction rate and effects on ultimate cumulative extraction; those effects in turn affect the extraction period. While the extra complexity may justify the use of numerical methods[49] (Gamponia and Mendelsohn, 1985), Heaps (1985) provides general analytical methods for the study of alternative taxes in such a context; Conrad and Hool (1981) deal with the issue of grade selection on a daily basis; Slade (1984) stresses the practical limits of theoretical results at the current level of generality.

The methodology must be altered so as to monitor both R and S simultaneously over time and at closure date. The extraction cost function is now $C(R, S)$ instead of $C(R)$, as in the general model of Section 1.2. By choice of $R(\cdot)$ and T, the competitive firm solves

$$Max \int_0^T e^{-rt}[p(t) R(t) - C(S(t), R(t))$$

$$- Z(S(t), R(t), p(t), t)]dt \qquad (5.9)$$

subject to

$$- dS/dt = R(t) \geq 0, \text{ with } S(0) = S_0 \text{ given.} \qquad (5.2)$$

In order to focus on Ricardian characteristics, $C(\cdot)$ and $C(\cdot) + Z(\cdot)$ are assumed to be such that complete exhaustion is uneconomic. Formally, whatever $p(t)$, there is a strictly positive level of S below which $pR - C(S, R) - Z(S, R, p, t) \leq 0$ for all R, including $\underline{R}(S)$ the extraction rate at which average cost, gross of tax, is minimum. The same regularity conditions apply as in the Hotelling case: p does not rise faster than at the discount rate; $C(\cdot) + Z(\cdot)$ is jointly concave in S, R for $R \geq R(s)$. The Hamiltonian is

$$H(\cdot) = e^{-rt}[(p - \mu)R - C(S, R) - Z(S, R, p, t)] \qquad (5.10)$$

Almost as in the Hotelling case, necessary conditions are

$$p = \mu + \partial C/\partial R + \partial Z/\partial R. \qquad (5.11)$$

---

[49] Numerical methods have also been used for the study of non-linear taxation, and tend to prevail in stochastic models (Mackie-Mason, 1987; Virmani, 1986).

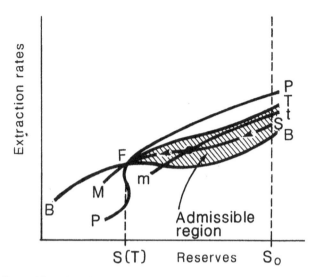

FIGURE 5.4 The Ricardian extraction model in (R, S) space.

$$d\mu/dt = r\mu + \partial C/\partial S + \partial Z/\partial S. \qquad (5.12)$$

One transversality condition at T requires the Hamiltonian to vanish which, combined with (5.11), in turn implies

$$(\partial/\partial R)[C(S,R)] + (\partial/\partial R)[Z(S,R,P(R),t)] \qquad (5.13)$$

$$= C(S,R)/R + Z(S,R,P(R),t)/R.$$

The second transversality condition is specific to the Ricardian model with incomplete exhaustion. Since $S(T) > 0$, $\mu(T) = 0$; combined with the condition that the Hamiltonian vanishes at T, it implies

$$P(R) = C(S,R)/R + Z(S,R,P(R),t)/R \text{ at } t = T. \qquad (5.14)$$

The analysis of this problem is more difficult than its Hotelling counterpart because $S(T)$ is now endogenous and $S(t)$ does not vanish from the relevant expressions as readily as before. Heaps (1985) provided a beautiful first treatment of a more general version of the problem. The methodology used now is slightly different from Heaps'.

Because the transversality conditions now specify both S and R it is necessary to characterize the solution in a (S, R) space rather than the convenient time space used above. In Figure 5.4, the BB locus represents the (S, R) pairs that satisfy (5.13). Thus on BB, for all relevant levels of S, R is such that average cost, inclusive of the tax, is minimized; its slope depends on the technology, the geology, and the tax system. The terminal point of the extraction program must be on BB. It must also satisfy (5.14), the condition that profits vanish at closure date. This condition is represented by locus PP, whose general shape and curvature is easily inferred from the assumptions on $C(\cdot) + Z(\cdot)$ and $P(\cdot)$: starting from BB, a change in R is a movement away from the (gross) cost minimizing rate; in order to maintain zero profits, S must increase accordingly. If p was unaffected by R in equilibrium, the PP locus would be vertical as it crosses BB; but since in general p diminishes as R rises, thus reducing profits, PP must have a finite positive slope at its inter-section with BB, at F. As it satisfies both (5.13) and (5.14), F is the terminal point for the extraction programme. At T, the programme must also satisfy (5.11), represented by the MT locus, whose slope at F is lower than that of PP because MT has the same relationship with PP as marginal cost with average cost, F being the point of minimum average cost. At other dates (5.11) must also be satisfied, but with $\mu > 0$; mt is one of the corresponding loci, which must cut BB further to the right of F, the higher μ. Now the solution can be characterized. The extraction path, represented by the arrowed line, must lie above BB (output above gross-cost minimizing rate), on the right of MT (μ is non-negative), start on the vertical through S_0 (initial reserves equal S_0), and end up at F. The higher the path, the higher the extraction rate, and the shorter the period necessary to use a given quantity of S. Note that the various loci in Figure 5.4 may shift over time if the problem is not time autonomous, that is if the tax function may shift over time.

Let us characterize the dynamics of the extraction path. Substituting the equilibrium condition $P(R) = p$ into (5.11), differentiating the resulting expression with respect to time, and using (5.11) and (5.12) to substitute for μ and $d\mu/dt$, one has

$$(dR/dt)[dP/dR - \partial^2C/\partial R^2 - \partial^2Z/\partial R^2 - (\partial^2Z/\partial R\partial p)(dP/dR)]$$
$$= r[p - \partial C/\partial R - \partial Z/\partial R] + \partial C/\partial S + \partial Z/\partial S$$
$$+ \partial^2Z/\partial R\partial t - (\partial^2C/\partial R\partial S + \partial^2Z/\partial R\partial S)R. \tag{5.15}$$

Since this differential equation is non-autonomous, its trajectories may cross in (R, S) space, making a qualitative analysis impossible in general in that space. Heaps provides conditions under which such crossing is

impossible in his model. As in most tax models, the price is taken as
exogenously given, and Heaps' conditions involve restrictions on its
trajectory combined with restrictions on the technology and the tax
environment. In the foregoing model, the assumption of a time autonomous demand schedule, combined with the market equilibrium requirement, suppress that source of time dependency. The sole source of time
dependency is the tax; it disappears when the tax parameters are constant
or time autonomous, as is the case in most practical applications and as
is assumed in the sequel unless otherwise mentioned.

Consider now alternative taxes, using, as before '*' subscripts to designate variables, functions, or expressions in the tax-free situation. The tax-
free situation is characterized by

$$(\partial/\partial R)[C(S^*, R^*)] = C(S^*, R^*)/R^* \text{ at } t = T^*, \quad (5.13^*)$$

$$P(R^*) = C(S^*, R^*)/R^* \text{ at } t = T^*, \quad (5.14^*)$$

$$(dR^*/dt)[dP/dR - \partial^2 C/\partial R^2] = r[p - \partial C/\partial R]$$
$$+ \partial C/\partial S - (\partial^2 C/\partial R \partial S)R. \quad (5.15^*)$$

A *franchise tax*, $Z = f$, leaves (5.15*) unaffected; thus the family of
possible trajectories from which the solution is selected is unchanged by
the tax and those trajectories do not cross in (R, S) space. However, both
terminal conditions are altered:

$$(\partial/\partial R)[C(S, R)] = C(S, R)/R + f/R. \quad (5.13f)$$

$$P(R) = C(S, R)/R + f/R \text{ at } t = T. \quad (5.14f)$$

It appears readily that the BB locus shifts up from B^*B^*, while the PP
locus shifts to the right from P^*P^*, as drawn in Figure 5.5. So the
franchise tax reduces the total amount of resource extracted ($S(T) >
S^*(T^*)$). Does it also speed up extraction as in the Hotelling case? The
answer depends on whether the SF curve lies above or below the S^*F^*
curve. Suppose the taxed curve SF lies below the tax free curve S^*F^*.
For the taxed programme, when reserves are down to $S(T)$, from
(5.11), $P(R) = \partial C(S(T), R)/\partial R + \partial Z/\partial R = \partial C(S(T), R)/\partial R$; this
is smaller than $\partial C(S(T), R^*)/\partial R$ by the assumption that $R^* > R$. But,
from (5.11*), $\partial C(S(T), R^*)/\partial R = P(R^*) - \mu^*$. Combining these
properties, $P(R) < P(R^*) - \mu^*$; but since $R^* > R$, $P(R^*) < P(R)$
which contradicts $\mu^* > 0$. Consequently, the SF trajectory must lie above
the S^*F^* trajectory, as drawn, a result conforming with the intuition that

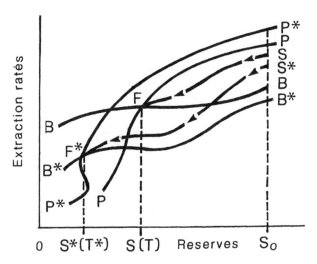

FIGURE 5.5 Ricardian model: effect of a franchise tax.

a given quantity of reserves will be extracted faster with a franchise tax because this reduces the period over which the tax is being paid and the total tax bill. This time inefficiency which was also observed in the Hotelling case comes in addition to the reduction in ultimate reserve extraction induced by the franchise tax in the Ricardian model.

With a *constant severance tax*, $Z(\cdot) = sR(t)$, terminal conditions (5.13) and (5.14) become

$$(\partial/\partial R)[C(S,R)] = C(S,R)/R. \qquad (5.13s)$$

$$P(R) = C(S,R)/R + s \text{ at } t = T. \qquad (5.14s)$$

Thus the BB locus is unchanged from $B*B*$ and the PP locus shifts to the right. As far as the dynamics of the solution path are concerned, (5.15) becomes

$$(dR/dt)[dP/dR - \partial^2 C/\partial R^2] = r[P - \partial C/\partial R - s] + \partial C/\partial S. \qquad (5.15s)$$

Suppose that the SF and the $S*F*$ paths did cross, unlike in Figure 5.6. At their intersection $dR/dt > dR*/dt$, which means that, in the (S,R) plan of Figure 5.6, SF would cut $S*F*$ from below. But, since $S*F*$ must

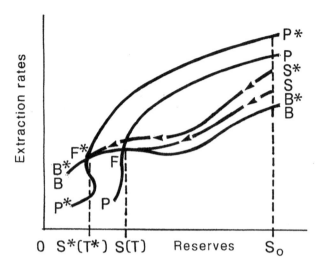

FIGURE 5.6 Ricardian model: effect of a constant severance or royalty.

lie everywhere above B^*B^* if extraction is to proceed at a rate higher than the average-cost-minimizing rate $R(S)$, and since B^*B^* is identical to BB, SF would have to cut S^*F^* again, this time from above, in order to reach its terminal point F on BB. This would contradict $dR/dt > dR^*/dt$[50]. Hence the SF path must not cut the S^*F^* path in Figure 5.6. The effects of the tax are now clear. There is a reduction in ultimate extraction. Since SF is below S^*F^*, it takes longer in the taxed case to extract any given amount of reserves; however, since the ultimate amount is reduced, T may be higher or lower than T^*. Similar results arise in the case of *ad valorem* severance taxes or royalties.

A property tax based on $S(t)$, $Z = gS(t)$, will shift BB up and PP to the right, since (5.13)* and (5.14)*, respectively, become

$$(\partial/\partial R)[C(S, R)] = C(S, R)/R + gS/R. \qquad (5.13g)$$

$$P(R) = C(S, R)/R + gs/R \text{ at } t = T. \qquad (5.14g)$$

Consequently, more reserves are left in the ground at closure. Instead of (5.15)*

---

[50]Heaps finds this to be a possibility in the case of a variable tax.

$$(dR/dt)[dP/dR - \partial^2 C/\partial R^2] = r[P - \partial C/\partial R] + \partial C/\partial S + g.$$
$$(5.15g)$$

Thus, if they cross, the paths must be such that $dR/dt < dR^*/dt$ at their intersection; SF must cut S^*F^* from above. But is this admissible? If it is, there may exist instances where a property tax slows down the extraction of a given amount of reserves. For example, in Figure 5.8, suppose that the tax is imposed when reserves are S_0' instead of S_0. Then, by the principle of optimality, the portion of the figure on the left of the vertical through S_0' still represents the solution to the new problem. For that new problem, the relevant part of S^*F^* is everywhere above the relevant part of SF which implies that the tax reduces the extraction rate relative to the tax free situation at any $S < S_0'$. This is counterintuitive as accelerated extraction is a way to avoid part of the tax burden. Let us show that this counterintuitive outcome is in fact ruled out. Suppose that the configuration of Figure 5.8 is possible. Then when $S = S(T)$ (and $\mu(T) = 0$), by (5.11), $\partial C(S(T), R)/\partial R = P(R)$ and, by (5.11)*, $P(R^*) = \partial CS(T), R^*)/\partial R + \mu^*$; since by assumption $R^* > R$, so that $P(R) > P(R^*)$, it follows that $\mu^* < \partial C(S(T), R)/\partial R - \partial C(S(T), R^*)/\partial R$, a difference which is itself negative by the assumption of rising marginal cost. But this implies $\mu^* < 0$, an impossibility. Thus the property tax reduces the ultimate amount of reserves extracted, and accelerates the rate at which those reserves are exploited, as represented in Figure 5.7; the counterintuitive configuration of Figure 5.8 is ruled out.

In the case of a *profit tax, possibly progressive*, $Z(\cdot) = u(\pi)\pi$, where $\pi = pR - C(S, R)$ and $u(\cdot)$ is non-decreasing, it is immediately apparent that the transversality conditions are not affected by the tax, so that the BB and PP loci stay at their tax free positions. Concerning the dynamics of the solution, (5.15) becomes

$$(dR/dt)[(dP/dR - \partial^2 C/\partial R^2)(1 - (\pi du/d\pi + u)) \qquad (5.15)\pi$$

$$- (\pi d^2 u/\partial d\pi^2 + 2du/d\pi)((\partial \pi/\partial R)^2 + R(dP/dR)(\partial \pi/\partial R))]$$

$$= [r(p - \partial C/\partial R) + \partial C/\partial S - R\partial^2 C/\partial R\partial S](1 - (\pi du/d\pi + u))$$

$$+ (\pi d^2 u/d\pi^2 + 2du/d\pi)[R(\partial \pi/\partial R)(\partial C/\partial S)].$$

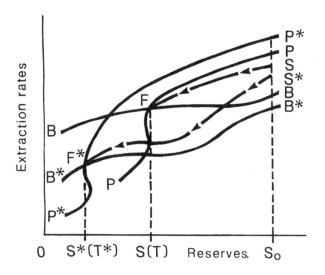

FIGURE 5.7 : Ricardian model: effect of an *ad valorem* property tax based on resource property value.

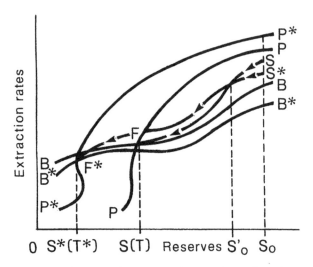

FIGURE 5.8 Ricardian model: an impossible configuration with *ad valorem* property tax.

This simplifies to $(5.15)^*$ if and only if $\pi d^2u/d\pi^2 + 2du/d\pi = 0$, which is the same neutrality condition (5.8) as in the Hotelling case. Again a progressive rate of return tax is not neutral unless it takes the form of a negative profit tax, linear in π and negative at low values of π. The effect of existing progressive rate of return taxes is not without ambiguity and depends on the particulars of the industries that are subject to it: technology, geology and demand conditions. With inefficient general taxation it is not surprising either that efficiency inducing resource taxation, as described by Hung and Long (1982), remains a theoretical proposition.

5.4 The corporate income tax

The corporate income tax is particular in two major respects. First it is actually a tax on capital income; its analysis requires the explicit introduction of capital in the model. Second, it is not specific to extractive sectors; on the contrary, as it affects most industries, its pressure is supposed to be spread evenly over an economy. The corporate income tax is a major element in most computations of effective tax rates; while these rates differ across countries and over time, one often expects them, according to the Schanz–Haig–Simons rule, to be identical for identical types of capital across sectors. But the corporate income tax contains special provisions for extractive firms. The most important and widespread of those provisions, the depletion allowance, is normally meant to reduce taxable income by the cost of the resource used over the period. Does it conform with the Schanz–Haig–Simons rule or with any alternative taxation principle? As will be argued below, neither its interpretation nor its rationale are very clear and its effect of reducing the effective tax rate in resource industries has been questioned repeatedly since Harberger (1955) criticized it.

Let us start with a partial efficiency analysis of the same type as in the previous subsection. In order to keep the model simple while endowing it with capital explicitly, assume that capital is the sole input and is fully malleable. If V is its asset price, its pre-tax rental price is

$$v = (r + \delta)V - dV/dt \qquad (5.16)$$

where δ is the physical depreciation rate. Reality can be further simplified by assuming that all investment is financed by retained earnings. Under this assumption, the discount rate is the same before, and after, tax and can be assumed to equal the exogenously given after-personal-income-tax interest rate.

Ignoring such features as the investment tax credit[51], the fundamental characteristics of the tax, besides its rate u, are the deductions involved in the definition of the tax base: the depreciation allowance, a proportion θ of the value of undepreciated capital C, aims at reflecting capital expenditures in the current period; the depletion allowance, a proportion β of the value of current extraction pR, aims at reflecting current non-renewable resource consumption. The tax is $u(pR - \beta pR - \theta C)$ and the firm chooses an investment programme $I(\cdot)$, thus also an extraction programme, to maximize the present value of its cumulative after-tax income flows. Omitting time arguments when no ambiguity arises the problem is

$$Max \int_0^T e^{-rt}[pR - VI - u(pR - \beta pR - \theta C)]\,dt$$
$$+ J(C(T),\, K(T),\, V(T)) \qquad (5.16)$$

subject to

$$dS/dt = -R;\ S(0) = S_0 \text{ given} \qquad (5.2)$$

$$dC/dt = VI - \theta C;\ C(0) = C_0 = V(0)K_0 \text{ given} \qquad (5.17)$$

$$dK/dt = I - \delta K;\ K(0) = K_0 \text{ given} \qquad (5.18)$$

$$R = F(S, K). \qquad (5.19)$$

(5.17) is the rule which specifies the book value of undepreciated capital for tax purposes. $J(\cdot)$ is the residual value of the firm at closure. It is the net result of selling any remaining capital at T and clearing with the tax authorities any discrepancy between $K(T)$ and $C(T)$; typically, since tax depreciation is usually faster than physical depreciation, the firm must reimburse the excess of tax depreciation over economic depreciation at T. $F(\cdot)$ is the production function, in a Ricardian model.

With malleable capital, if the tax provisions at closure amount to a continuation of previous provisions with respect to depreciation (see Gaudet and Lasserre, 1984), then problem (5.16) is equivalent, as in

---

[51]The investment tax credit can easily be incorporated into the analysis; I choose here not to complicate the notation.

the literature based on Jorgenson (1963), to a problem involving the direct choice of $K(\cdot)$, where the services of K are paid at their before-tax rental rate v

$$Max \int_0^T e^{-rt}[pR - C(S,R) - u(pR - zC(S,R) - \beta pR)]dt$$

(5.20)

subject to (5.2)

where $C(S,R) \equiv vK(S,R)$, $K(S,R)$ being the input requirement function associated with the production function (5.19); and $z = \theta/(r+\theta)$ is the present value of a dollar of undepreciated capital which can be depreciated indefinitely at rate θ.

(5.20) is a particular case of (5.9), so that the corporate income tax can now undergo a similar analysis as the taxes studied in the previous subsection. The comparison between the tax-free situation and the programme under corporate income tax is further facilitated if one divides through by $(1 - uz)$, assumed constant, to get the equivalent problem

$$Max \int_0^T e^{-rt}[\alpha pR - C(S,R)]dt$$

(5.21)

subject to (5.2)

where $\alpha \equiv [1 - (1 - \beta)u]/(1 - uz)$. Since (5.21) differs from the tax-free problem by the output price only, its solution is described by (5.13)*, (5.14)* and (5.15)* where p or $P(R)$, and dP/dR, are respectively replaced by αp, $\alpha P(R)$, and $\alpha dP/dR$. Locus BB, which will be remembered to represent pairs (S,R) such that R minimizes gross average cost, is unaffected by the tax and remains identical to B^*B^*. Locus PP, representing the zero profit condition which must also be satisfied at T, lies to the right (left) of P^*P^* if $\alpha > 1(<1)$. Finally, comparing (5.15)* with its taxed version, if the trajectories for (S^*, R^*) and (S,R) pairs were to cross they would be such that, at their intersection,

$$dR/dt = dR^*/dt - (\alpha - 1)(dP/dR)/[(dP/dR) - \partial^2C/\partial R^2].$$

(5.22)

This makes an intersection of SF and S^*F^* in Figure 5.9 impossible. Indeed, suppose that $\alpha < 1$ so that F lies on the right of F^*. (5.22)

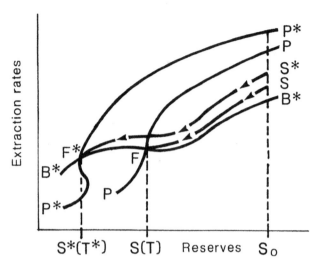

FIGURE 5.9 Ricardian model: corporate income tax, $\alpha < 1$

implies $dR/dt > dR^*/dt$, which means that SF cuts S^*F^* from below. But this is an impossible configuration if SF is to terminate at F, below S^*F^*. It follows that SF is everywhere below S^*F^*, as drawn, if $\alpha < 1$, which means that the tax causes less reserve to be extracted, and at a slower rate. Conversely, SF lies everywhere above S^*F^*, with F on the left of F^*, if $\alpha > 1$. Neutrality arises if $\alpha = 1$. Inspecting the formula for α, it is clear that α reflects the tax treatment of K, as measured by z, the value of 1\$ of investment in future tax depreciations, relative to the tax treatment of the resouce, as measured by β. The depletion allowance may be used to adjust the tax treatment of the resource so as to balance the tax treatment of capital in such a way as to eliminate the distortions resulting from the corporate income tax. This requires setting $\beta = 1 - z$; the more favourable the treatment of capital, the less favourable the depletion allowance should be. One type of capital has to be taxed more heavily when the other type is taxed lightly, in order to leave the overall production incentive unaffected. This result, derived here for the Ricardian case, also applies to a Hotelling resource (Gaudet and Lasserre, 1984).

The focus on neutrality in a partial equilibrium set-up represents a narrow point of view as resource sectors are just some among many others in the economy and as several taxes, the corporate income tax in particular, affect both resource industries and other industries. In a second-best world, when other sectors are subject to distorting taxation, it is more meaningful to compare the tax treatments of various sectors and inputs than to wonder about tax neutrality in resource industries alone. Gaudet and Lasserre (1986) have discussed the corporate income tax and the depletion allowance from that point of view for a Hotelling resource. They define a hypothetical tax which collects a proportion τ of true capital income in non-extractive sectors and a proportion τ^e in extractive sectors. True capital income is defined as $pR - \delta VK$ in a non-extractive sector, where R is interpreted as output not subject to any resource constraint; in extractive sectors, true capital income is $pR - \delta VK - \eta R$, where η is the value of the *in situ* resource. Then they compute the values of τ and τ^e at which the hypothetical taxes have the same real effects as the corporate income tax on non-extractive sectors and extractive sectors, respectively. Those values of τ and τ^e represent both marginal and average effective rates of the corporate income tax. Gaudet and Lasserre find that, given the other parameters of the corporate income tax, the depletion allowance can be selected in a way which equalizes effective tax rates on capital income in extractive and non-extractive sectors. This result is achieved when the depletion allowance is precisely set at the value of *in situ* resource consumption, i.e. for $\beta = \mu/p$. The common effective tax rate is then

$$\tau = \tau^e = (u - uz)/[1 - uz - (1 - u)\delta V/v]. \qquad (5.23)$$

The same result is valid for the Ricardian model, as is shown now.

Let the hypothetical tax on true capital income apply the same effective rate τ, given by (5.23), in all extractive and non-extractive sectors. The corporate income tax is equivalent to the hypothetical tax if extraction rates are identical under both regimes. Those programmes must satisfy (5.11)c and (5.11)τ, where 'c' and 'τ' refer to corporate-income-tax and pure-capital-income-tax situations, respectively. The former is obtained in solving problem (5.20) the usual way

$$p(1 - u)/(1 - uz) - \mu^c\{[1 - u(\beta p/\mu^c)]/(1 - uz)\} = \partial C/\partial R$$
$$(5.11c)$$

where μ^c is the *in situ* value of the resource under the corporate income tax.

Similarly, in order to obtain (5.11)τ, one must solve the problem of the firm under the hypothetical tax on true capital income $\tau(pR - \delta VK - \eta R)$ where η is the true value of the *in situ* resource under the tax. As with (5.20), that problem is equivalent to

$$Max \int_0^T e^{-rt}[pR - vK(S,R) - \tau(pR - \delta VK(S,R) - \eta R)]\,dt$$

$$(5.24)$$

subject to (5.2)

As a necessary condition one has

$$p(1 - \tau)/(1 - \tau\delta V/v) - \mu^\tau[1 - \tau/(1 - \tau\delta V/v)] = \partial C/\partial R$$

where the fact that η represents the true value of the *in situ* resource has been used to set it equal to the shadow price μ^τ. With τ given by (5.23), this gives

$$p(1 - u)/(1 - uz) - \mu^\tau(1 - u)/(1 - uz) = \partial C/\partial R$$

$$(5.11\tau)$$

(5.11)τ and (5.11)c will be identical at all dates if $\beta p/\mu^c = 1$ and $\mu^c = \mu^\tau$ at all dates. If the first condition is imposed by setting $\beta = \mu^c/p$ at all dates, it can be verified by further characterizing the solutions of both problems (5.20) and (5.24) that the second condition indeed also will be satisfied. This completes the proof that a depletion allowance equal to the true value of current reserve consumption ensures the equality of effective tax rates in extractive and non-extractive corporate sectors. While existing versions of the depletion allowance involve a constant rate β, so that they can only approach such an outcome, effective tax rate uniformity across sectors is apparently the rationale for this special provision of the corporate income tax. As argued below, it is hard to find any such rationale for the provisions of the corporate income tax with respect to exploration.

5.5 Exploration

The issue of exploration has been deliberately ignored so far. Initial reserves were treated as exogenously given and the focus was on decisions having to do with the best exploitation of existing reserves, the so-called intensive margin (Livernois and Uhler, 1987). In reality, reserves are the result of prior exploration efforts and are largely endogenous. Their determination is governed by decisions at what is known as the extensive margin. Although widely recognized, the effect of taxation at the extensive margin has not received the same thorough treatment as its effect at the intensive margin. As a simplified, but enlightening, way to look at this process, assume that the extraction phase studied so far is preceded by an exploration period of endogenous duration over which the firm extends exploration efforts to progressively accumulate the stock S_0. Extraction starts up when exploration is over, which can be viewed as a simplification of reality. The start-up date is endogenous; however, since the durations of both the extraction and the exploration periods are themselves endogenous, there is no loss of generality in using the convention that the start-up date is $t = 0^{52}$.

In this extended problem, the firm must select in a first phase its flows of exploration inputs and, in a second phase, its flows of extraction inputs, in such a way as to maximize net cumulative discounted revenues from extraction, minus cumulative compounded exploration expenditures, net of taxes

$$Max \int_0^T e^{-rt}[pR - C(S, R) - Z(\cdot)]dt - EX(S_0) \qquad (5.25)$$

subject to

$$- dS/dt = R(t) \text{ with } S_0 \text{ endogenous} \qquad (5.2)$$

and

$$EX(S_0) \text{ defined by } (5.26)$$

$EX(S_0)$ is the optimized value of cumulative net of tax exploration expenditures, obtained by selecting exploration inputs so as to

$$Min \int_{-T_x}^0 e^{-rt} ex(s, S) dt \qquad (5.26)$$

subject to

---

[52]This would not be so if the problem was not time-autonomous.

$$dS/dt = s(-t) \text{ with } S(-T_x) = 0 \text{ and } S(0) = S_0 \qquad (5.27)$$

s is the rate of discoveries; $ex(\cdot)$ is the after-tax cost of discoveries, rising and convex in s, non-decreasing in S (Lasserre, 1985a; Devarajan and Fisher, 1982); $-T_x$ is the endogenous date at which exploration activities begin. Problem (5.26) is formally similar to a Ricardian mining problem with this difference that, instead of optimally depleting a reserve stock, the firm optimally builds such a stock up to the target level S_0. As was done in the analysis of the extraction problem, it is possible to make a distinction between a Hotelling view of exploration, where cumulative discoveries do not cause any shift in discovery costs $(\partial ex(\cdot)/\partial S = 0)$, and a Ricardian view, where discoveries become more costly as S increases $(\partial ex(\cdot)/\partial S > 0)$[53]. The corresponding value function $EX(S_0)$ is convex and rising in either case.

When S_0 is given, problem (5.25) reduces to the tax problem studied earlier, since $EX(S_0)$ is a constant in that case. When S_0 is endogenous, the transversality condition which must be satisfied at $t = 0$ is

$$\mu(0) = dEX(\cdot)/dS. \qquad (5.28)$$

It says that the shadow value, for extraction purposes, of the marginal unit of *in situ* reserves, must equal the marginal cost of producing it at the end of the exploration phase. As pointed out by Lasserre (1985a) this marginal cost is inclusive of the rent that unexplored land might command.

It is now possible to study the effect of taxation on exploration by examining the impact of alternative taxes on (5.28). With the exception of the corporate income tax, the taxes examined above do not affect exploration costs; they leave the right-hand side of (5.28) unaffected. But to the extent that they do tax extraction, they reduce μ on average and, in most instances, it can be shown that $\mu(0)$ is reduced. As a result the optimal level of S_0 is reduced; mining taxes cause a contraction at the extensive margin.

---

[53]For a stochastic formulation of the Hotelling view, see Arrow and Chiang (1982), and Lasserre (1984a); for a stochastic formulation of the Ricardian view, see Lasserre (1985b).

The case of the corporate income tax is more complex. In most countries, the corporate income tax includes special provisions for exploration expenditures. Often those are immediately deductible against income from other resource operations so that, in most instances, the after-tax cost of one dollar of exploration expenditures is $\$(1 - u)$. Assuming this to be the case in the foregoing model, the relation between net compounded cumulative exploration expenditures under corporate income tax and in the absence of tax is $EX(S) = (1 - u)EX^*(S)$. As a result

$$dEX/dS = (1 - u)dE^*/dS.$$

Having determined the effect of the tax on the right-hand side of (5.28), it remains to verify whether, for any given S_0, the tax reduces μ in a smaller or in a greater proportion. While it is difficult in general to compute μ and μ^* explicitly to find out, it can be shown that a pure rent tax at a rate ϕ is neutral and reduces the resource rent to a proportion[54] $(1 - \phi)$ of its original value. As shown above, when β is set equal to $1 - z$, the corporate income tax is such a tax. Indeed when $\beta = 1 - z$ the objective functional in (5.20) reduces to

$$Max \int_0^T e^{-rt}(1 - uz)[pR - C(S, R)]dt$$

so that the rate of the pure rent tax in that case is uz and

$$\mu = (1 - uz)\mu^*.$$

This shows that, in the benchmark case of a neutral corporate income tax, the left-hand side of (5.28) is reduced in a smaller proportion than the right-hand side. The tax induces a higher level of exploration in that case. In tax regimes that depart from the neutral case, this expansion at the extensive margin is likely to be less acute, the more favourable the treatment of extraction activities relative to exploration activities.

Of course, given the uncertainty associated with exploration, results obtained within a non-stochastic framework must be considered only indicative. Campbell and Lindner (1983, 1985a, 1985b) have attempted a stochastic treatment of the resource rent tax. They focus on

---

[54]The neutral royalty presented above in a Hotelling model is an example of this property.

exploration, with full or partial loss offset and with risk-neutral or risk-averse firms. Exploration is modelled as a costly process which yields information on the value of incompletely known deposits. Once the optimum level of information has been acquired, the deposit is exploited or abandoned. Here tax provisions with respect to loss offset turn out to matter. The authors find that the resource rent tax with full loss offset is neutral with respect to exploration effort, as in the non-stochastic set-up, if firms are risk neutral. With risk-averse firms, an increase in the rate of resource rent tax with full loss offset results in the taxing authority bearing a greater share of project risk. Because this amounts to a reduction in the firm's degree of risk aversion, promising deposits are explored less and unpromising ones are explored more. With partial loss offset neutrality is lost even when the firms are risk neutral.

Leland (1978), and Hyde and Markusen (1985), apply an optimal-taxation approach to the same problem, also cast into a two-period static mould. There are two levels of uncertainty. First, the firm must determine whether or not there is a deposit in a given track of land; if there is one, the probability of finding it depends on exploration expenditures. Second, once the result of exploration activities is known, there remains uncertainty about the size of reserves, and the firm must select production expenditures in that context. The government is completely informed about the firms, although it may differ from them in its *ex-ante* and *ex-post* assessments of uncertainty[55]. It selects a set of tax instruments in order to achieve three targets: optimal level of exploration activity; optimal level of extraction activity; some pre-specified distribution of expected resource rents. The first two tax instruments can easily be related to the above analysis of the corporate income tax: they specify in what proportions the government and firms share exploration costs, as well as production costs and revenues. The third instrument specifies the state dependent bonus bid that firms will agree to submit, if they behave competitively, in order to secure the right to exploit the parcel[56]. Since the government shares equally in production expenditures and revenues, this amounts to a pure *ex-post*

---

[55] In that sense there may be disagreement. However, the differences being public knowledge, there is no information asymmetry.

[56] Note that in practice, bonus bids are not state dependent. For an extended empirical and theoretical discussion and bibliography on the subject, see Ramsey (1980).

rent tax. However, unlike the certainty case, optimality is not generally compatible with the absence of a bonus bid. The latter has the role of redistributing wealth across states in such a way that a firm's expected marginal utility is constant across states. Such redistribution is not needed if the firms are risk-neutral; in that case, the pure rent tax is optimal, and neutral, in the absence of any state dependent bonus bid, as in Campbell and Lindner and as in the non-stochastic model analysed earlier. With respect to the *ex-ante* exploration decision, Hyde and Markusen point out that both the government and firms benefit from exploration activities, since they are going to share in the proceeds; as a result, the marginal condition for optimal exploration is similar to a Lindahl pricing rule, involving the sum of government and firm expected marginal utilities, as with any public good. In a non-stochastic framework, this explains why, according to (5.28), neutrality arises when the tax system affects exploration expenditures in the same proportion as the resource rent. However, because government and firm incomes move in opposite directions, this simple result no longer holds in a stochastic environment with risk aversion, unless agents have identical constant risk aversions and hold identical subjective probability distributions.

5.6 Optimal taxation and tax incidence in general equilibrium

Optimal taxation issues have crept repeatedly into the previous sections, although I tried to confine the analysis to more descriptive aspects and criteria, using concepts such as neutrality and distorting effects, or effective tax rates, rather than optimality. Indeed, as Simons (1977) and Long and Sinn (1984) have reasserted, the problem of optimal natural resource taxation is a second-best problem. As such it must be studied within the proper general equilibrium framework.

As was shown above, a depletion allowance is the resource analogue of true economic depreciation; for the particular form of corporate income tax studied earlier, it ensures the equalization of effective tax rates across all corporate sectors in the economy. Because it corresponds to the Haig–Simons rule and ensures the equality of marginal products across sectors, this particular system has been advocated, among others, by Dasgupta, Heal and Stiglitz (1980). However Long and Sinn give an example where it is suboptimal to extend this rule to extractive sectors when it is already applied to the rest of the economy.

In their three-sector example, consumers are taxed on their interest income and equate the marginal rate of time preference to the net-of-tax rate of interest while, for firms, the depletion allowance equates the return from holding the resource with the gross rate of interest. In equilibrium, this results in too rapid an extraction rate. In the model of Long and Sinn, an efficient second-best tax on the extractive firm is a tax on real cash flow where the tax rate equals that on interest income and interest is tax-deductible. Clearly, this result is dependent on the treatment of consumers relative to firms in the given tax set-up. For example, if firms are financed by retained earnings and dividends are taxed at the same rate as other sources of income, the consumer rate of time preference is equal to the after-tax discount rate of firms; in that case it is probably optimal to extend the Schanz–Haig–Simons rule to extractive sectors.

Tax incidence also belongs to the realm of general equilibrium analysis. Resources have generally been ignored in theoretical incidence analyses à la Harberger (1962), although taxes and subsidies are generally key features of resource sectors. Recently, however, the use of computable general equilibrium models has brought new results in this important area; an extensive bibliography is to be found in Decaluwé and Martens (1988) and Hertel (1988) discusses the theoretical issues involved and their empirical relevance. Those contributions share a major deficiency: neither of them incorporates the dynamics of resource depletion.

Competitive equilibrium is not always the appropriate equilibrium framework for the analysis of resource taxation. Strategic behaviour on the part of countries or jurisdictions may play an important role, as resource finiteness, in quantity and number of locations, reduces the number of actors. With the obvious analogy of the Opec cartel in mind, Brander and Spencer (1984), and Bergstrom (1982), have shown how non-cooperative international policy equilibrium could be characterized by export cartels and rent-extracting tariffs set by importing countries. In other circumstances, two producer areas under different jurisdictions may compete for sales on a common market. Using the example of coal in Wyoming and Montana, Kolstad and Wolak (1983) study a duopoly model where the duopolists are the governments of each coal state, competing with tax instruments. As is often the case in duopoly models of resource extraction, exhaustibility is not treated as an explicit factor, the model is static. Nonetheless, the authors derive the appropriate tax reaction functions and the resulting equilibrium, under the assumption of Cournot-Nash competition. They also investigate Stackelberg behaviour. The model is then used to compute numerically the tax rates that would prevail under alternative assumptions in each state.

BIBLIOGRAPHY

Agbeyegbe, T. D. (1989), 'Interest Rates and Metal Price Movements: Further Evidence', *Journal of Environmental Economics and Management* **16(2)**, 184–92.
Arrow, K. and S. Chang (1982), 'Optimal Pricing Use and Exploration of Uncertain Natural Resource Stocks', *Journal of Environmental Economics and Management* **9(1)**, 1–10.
Barnett, H. J. (1979), 'Scarcity and Growth Revisited', in Smith, V. K. (ed.), *Scarcity and Growth Reconsidered*, Johns Hopkins University Press (for *Resources for the Future*), Baltimore.
Barnett, H. J. and C. Morse (1963), *Scarcity and Growth: The Economics of Natural Resource Availability*, Johns Hopkins University Press, Baltimore.
Baumol, W. J. and W. E. Oates (1975), *The Theory of Environmental Policy*, Prentice-Hall, Englewood Cliffs, New Jersey.
Benzoni, L. (1988) 'Sur la portée de la théorie hotellinienne des ressources épuisables', *Revue d'économie politique* **98(1)**, 159–73.
Bergstrom, T. C. (1982), 'On Capturing Oil Rents with a National Excise Tax', *American Economic Review* **72(1)**, 194–201.
Blackorby, C. and W. Schworm (1984), 'The Structure of Economics with Aggregate Measures of Capital: a Complete Characterization', *Review of Economic Studies* **51(4)**, 633–50.
Boskin, M. J., M. S. Robinson, T. O'Reilly and P. Kumar (1985), 'New Estimates of the Value of Federal Mineral Rights and Land', *American Economic Review* **75(5)**, 923–936.
Brander, J. A. and B. J. Spencer (1984), 'Trade Warfare: Tariffs and Cartels', *Journal of International Economics* **16(3/4)**, 227–242.
Buchanan, J. M. and G. Tullock (1975), 'Polluters' Profits and Political Response: Direct Controls versus Taxes', *American Economic Review* **65**, 139–147.
Burness, H. S. (1976), 'The Taxation of Non-renewable Natural Resources', *Journal of Environmental Economics and Management* **3**, 289–311.
Cairns, R. D. (1981), 'An Application of Depletion Theory to a Base Metal: Canadian Nickel', *Canadian Journal of Economics* **14(4)**, 635–648.
Cairns, R. D. (1986), 'A Model of Exhaustible Resource Exploitation with Ricardian Rent', *Journal of Environmental Economics and Management* **13**, 313–24.
Cairns, R. D. (1991), 'The Economics of Exploration for Non-Renewable Resources: an Interpretive Survey', *Journal of Economic Surveys*, forthcoming.
Cairns, R. D. (1990a), 'Geological Influences, Metal Prices and Rationality', *Resources and Energy*, **12**, 143–71.
Cairns, R. D. (1990b), 'A Contribution to the Theory of Depletable Resource Scarcity and its Measures', *Economic Enquiry*, **28(4)**, 744–55.
Cairns, R. D. and P. Lasserre (1986), 'Sectoral Supply of Minerals of Varying Grade', *Scandinavian Journal of Economics* **88(4)**, 605–626.
Campan, E. and A. Grimaud (1988), 'Le syndrome Hollandais', rapport technique no 8810, GREMAQ, Université de Toulouse I, France.

Campbell, H.F. (1980), 'The Effect of Capital Intensity on the Optimal Rate of Extraction of a Mineral Deposit' *Çanadian Journal of Economics* **13(2)**, 349–55.

Campbell, H.F. and R.K. Lindner (1983), 'On the Optimal Resource Rent Tax', *Economic Letters* **13**, 263–268.

Campbell, H.F. and R.K. Lindner (1985a), 'Mineral Exploration and the Neutrality of Real Royalties', *Economic Record* (March), 445–449.

Campbell, H.F. and R.K. Lindner (1985b), 'A Model of Mineral Exploration and Resource Taxation', *Economic Journal* **95(3)**, 146–160.

Chichilnisky, G. (1986), 'Prix du pétrole, prix industriels et production: une analyse macroéconomique d'équilibre général', in Gaudet, G. and P. Lasserre, eds.

Chichilnisky, G., G. Heal and D. McLeod (1986), 'Ressources naturelles, commerce et endettement', in Gaudet, G. and P. Lasserre, eds.

Conrad, R.F. and B. Hool (1980), *Taxation of Mineral Resources*, Lexington Books, Lexington.

Conrad, R.F. and B. Hool (1981), 'Resource Taxation with Heterogeneous Quality and Endogenous Reserves', *Journal of Public Economics* **16**, 17–33.

Corden, M.W. (1984), 'Booming Sector and Dutch Disease Economics: Survey and Consolidation', *Oxford Economic Papers* **36**, 359–380.

Crabbé, P.J. (1983), 'The Contribution of L.C. Gray to Economic Theory of Exhaustible Natural Resources and its Roots in the History of Economic Thought', *Journal of Environmental Economics and Management* **10**, 195–220.

Dasgupta, P.S. (1982), *The Control of Resources*, Basil Blackwell Publications Ltd., Oxford.

Dasgupta, P.S. and G.M. Heal (1974), 'The Optimal Depletion of Exhaustible Resources', *Review of Economic Studies*, Symposium on the Economics of Exhaustible Resources, 3–28.

Dasgupta, P.S. and G.M. Heal (1979), *Economic Theory and Exhaustible Resources*, James Nisbet and Co. Ltd., Digswell Place and Cambridge University Press.

Dasgupta, P.S. and J.E. Stiglitz (1981), 'Resource Depletion under Technological Uncertainty, *Econometrica* **49**, 85–104.

Dasgupta, P.S., G.M. Heal and J.E. Stiglitz (1980), 'The Taxation of Exhaustible Resources', in Hughes, G.A. and G.M. Heal, eds., *Public Policy and the Tax System*, George Allen and Unwin, London.

Dasgupta, P.S., R. Gilbert and J. Stiglitz (1983), 'Strategic Considerations in Invention and Innovation: The Case of Natural Resources', *Econometrica* **51(5)**, 1439–1448.

Dea, C., P. Lasserre and P. Ouellette (1988), 'Prix des ressources et règle d'Hotelling', 25th International Conference of the Applied Econometrics Association, Washington, D.C.

Decaluwé, B. and A. Martens (1988), 'Bibliographie relative aux modèles calculables d'équilibre général appliqués aux économies en développement', Cahier no 1188, Centre de recherche et développement en économique, Université de Montréal.

Deshmukh, S.D. and S.R. Pliska (1980), 'Optimal Consumption and Exploration of Non-renewable Resources under Uncertainty', *Econometrica* **48(1)**, 177–200.

Deshmukh, S.D. and S.R. Pliska (1983), 'Optimal Consumption of a Nonrenewable Resource with Stochastic Discoveries and a Random Environment', *Review of Economic Studies* **50(3)**, 543–554.

Devarajan, S. and A.C. Fisher (1982), 'Exploration and Scarcity', *Journal of Political Economy* **90(6)**, 1279–1290.

Dodds, D. and R.C. Bishop (1983), 'On the Role of Information in Mineral Exploration', *Land Economics* **59(4)**, 411–417.

Eswaran, M. and T.R. Lewis (1984a), 'Appropriability and the Extraction of a Common property Resource' *Economica* **51(204)**, 393–400.

Eswaran, M. and T. R. Lewis (1984b), 'Ultimate Recovery of an Exhaustible Resource Under Different Market Structures', *Journal of Environmental Economics and Management* 11(1), 55–69.

Eswaran, M., T. R. Lewis and T. Heaps (1983), 'On the Non-existence of Market Equilibria in Exhaustible Resource Markets with Decreasing Costs', *Journal of Political Economy* 91(1), 155–167.

Farrow, S. (1985), 'Testing the Efficiency of Extraction from a Stock Resource', *Journal of Political Economy* 93(3), 452–487.

Fisher, A. (1981), *Resources and Environmental Economics*, Cambridge University Press.

Forsyth, P. J. (1986), 'Booming Sectors and Structural Change in Australia and Britain: A Comparison', in Neary, J. P. and S. Van Wijnbergen, eds.

Gaffney, M. (1967), *Extractive Resources and Taxation*, University of Wisconsin Press, Madison.

Gamponia, V. and R. Mendelsohn (1985), 'The Taxation of Exhaustible Resources', *Quarterly Journal of Economics*, 165–181.

Garnaut, R. and A. C. Ross (1975), 'Uncertainty, Risk Aversion, and the Taxing of Natural Resources', *Economic Journal* 85, 272–287.

Garnaut, R. and A. C. Ross (1979), 'The Neutrality of the Resource Rent Tax', *Economic Record* 55(150), 193–201.

Gaudet, G. (1983), 'Investissement optimal et Coûts d'adjustement dans la théorie économique de la mine', *Revue canadienne d'économique* 16(1), 39–51.

Gaudet, G. and P. Howitt (1989), 'A Note on Uncertainty and Hotelling Rule', *Journal of Environmental Economics and Management,* 16(1), 80–86.

Gaudet, G. and A. M. Khadr (1991) 'The Evolution of Natural Resource Prices under Stochastic Investment Opportunities: An Intertemporal Asset-Pricing Approach', *International Economic Review*, forthcoming.

Gaudet, G. and P. Lasserre (1984), 'L'impôt sur le revenu des sociétés et le coût du capital pour l'entreprise minière', *Revue canadienne d'économique* 17(4), 778–787.

Gaudet, G. and P. Lasserre (1986), 'Capital Income Taxation, Depletion Allowances, and Non-renewable Resource Extraction', *Journal of Public Economics* 29, 241–253.

Gaudet, G. and P. Lasserre (1988), 'On Comparing Monopoly and Competition in Exhaustible Resource Exploitation', *Journal of Environmental Economics and Management* 15(4), 412–418.

Gelb, A. H. (1986), 'Adjustment to Windfall Gains: A Comparative Analysis of Oil-exporting Countries', in Neary, J. P. and S. Van Wijnbergen, eds.

Gilbert, R. J. (1979), 'Optimal Depletion of an Uncertain Stock' *Review of Economic Studies* 46, 45–57.

Gray, L. C. (1914), 'Rent Under the Assumption of Exhaustibility', *Quarterly Journal of Economics* 28, 466–489.

Hahn, F. H. (1966), 'Equilibrium Dynamics with Heterogeneous Capital Goods', *Quarterly Journal of Economics* 88, 65–94.

Hall, D. C. and J. V. Hall (1984), 'Concepts and Measures of Natural Resource Scarcity with a Summary of Recent Trends', *Journal of Environmental Economics and Management* 11, 363–379.

Halvorsen, R. and T. R. Smith (1984), 'On Measuring Natural Resource Scarcity', *Journal of Political Economy* 92(5), 954–964.

Halvorsen, R. and T. R. Smith (1987), 'A Test of the Theory of Exhaustible Resources', mimeo, University of Washington, Seattle.

Hanson, D. A. (1980), 'Increasing Extraction Costs and Resource Prices: Some Further Results', *The Bell Journal of Economics* 11(1), 335–342.

Harberger, A.C. (1955), 'Taxation of Mineral Industries', reprinted in Harberger, A.C. (1974), *Taxation and Welfare*, Little, Brown and Company, Boston.

Harberger, A.C. (1962), 'The Incidence of the Corporate Income Tax', *Journal of Political Economy* **70**, 215–240.

Hartwick, J.M. (1978), 'Exploitation of Many Deposit of an Exhaustible Resource', *Econometrica* **46(1)**, 201–217.

Hartwick, J.M. and N. Oleweiler (1986), *The Economics of Natural Resource Use*, Harper and Row Publishers, New York.

Hartwick, J.M. and P. Sadorsky (1990) 'Duopoly in Exhaustible Resource Exploration and Extraction', *Canadian Journal of Economics* **23(2)**, 276–93.

Heal, G. and M. Barrow (1980), 'Relationship Between Interest Rates and Metal Price Movements', *Review of Economic Studies* **47**, 161–181.

Heaps, T. (1985), 'The Taxation of Nonreplenishable Natural Resources Revisited', *Journal of Environmental Economics and Management* **12(1)**, 14–27.

Heaps, T. and J.F. Helliwell (1985), 'The Taxation of Natural Resources', in Auerbach, A. and M. Feldstein, eds., *Handbook of Public Economics*, North Holland, Amsterdam.

Helliwell, J.F. (1981), 'Using Canadian Oil and Gas Revenues in the 1980's: Provincial and Federal Perspectives' in T. Barber and V. Brailovsky, eds., *Oil or Industry?*, Academic Press, London.

Herfindahl, O.C. (1967), 'Depletion and Economic Theory', in Gaffney, M., ed.

Hertel, T.W. (1988), 'General Equilibrium Incidence of Natural Resource Subsidies: The Three Factor Case', *Journal of Environmental Economics and Management* **15(2)**, 206–223.

Hillman, A.L. and N.V. Long (1985), 'Monopolistic Recycling of Oil Revenue and Intertemporal Bias in Depletion and Trade', *Quarterly Journal of Economy* **99**, 598–624.

Hoel, M. (1978a), 'Resource Extraction, Substitute Production, and Resource Monopoly', *Journal of Economic Theory* **19(1)**, 28–37.

Hoel, M. (1978b), 'Resource Extraction and Recycling with Environmental Costs', *Journal of Environmental Economics and Management* **5**, 220–235.

Hoel, M. (1981), 'Resource Extraction by a Monopolist with Influence Over the Rate of Return on Non-resource Assets', *International Economic Review* **22(1)**, 147–157.

Hoel, M. (1983), 'Monopoly Resource Extractions Under the Presence of Predetermined Substitute Production', *Journal of Economic Theory* **30(1)**, 201–212.

Hoel, M. (1984), 'Extraction of a Resource with a Substitute for Some of its Uses', *Canadian Journal of Economics* **17(3)**, 593–602.

Hotelling, H. (1931), 'The Economics of Exhaustible Resources', *Journal of Political Economy* **39(2)**, 137–175.

Hung, N.M. (1986), 'On Simultaneous Extraction from Several Resource Deposits', Cahier no 8619, Départment d'économique, Université Laval.

Hung, N.M., M.C. Kemp, and N.V. Long (1984), 'On the Transition from an Exhaustible-resource Stock to an Inexhaustible Substitute', in Kemp, M.C. and N.V. Long, eds.

Hung, N.M. and N.V. Long (1982), 'Efficiency-inducing Taxation for a Monopolistically-supplied Depletable Resource: The Case of Stock-dependent Extraction Cost', in Kemp, M.C. and N.V. Long, eds.

Hyde, R. and J.R. Markusen (1982), 'Exploration Versus Extraction Costs as Determinants of Optimal Mineral Rights Leases', *Economic Record* **58(162)**, 224–234.

Jevons, W.S. (1865), *The Coal Question*, 3rd edition (1906), MacMillan and Co., London.

Johanson, P.O. (1987), *The Economic Theory and Measurement of Environment Benefits*, Cambridge University Press.

Jones, R.W. and P.R. Kenen (1984), *Handbook of International Economics*, Vol. I, Elsevier Science Publishers, Amsterdam.

Jorgenson, D.W. (1963), 'Capital Theory and Investment Behavior', *American Economic Review* 53, 247–259.

Kemp, M.C. (1976), 'How to Eat a Cake of Unknown Size' in *Three Topics in the Theory of International Trade: Distribution, Welfare, and Uncertainty*, North Holland, Amsterdam.

Kemp, M.C. and N.V. Long (1980a), 'A Modest Defense of the Use of Cobb-Douglas Production Functions in the Analysis of Exhaustible Resources', in Kemp, M.C. and N.V. Long, eds.

Kemp, M.C. and N.V. Long, eds. (1980b), *Exhaustible Resources, Optimality and Trade*, North Holland Publishing Company, Amsterdam.

Kemp, M.C. and N.V. Long (1980c), 'On the Optimal Order of Exploitation of Deposits of an Exhaustible Resource', in Kemp and Long, eds.

Kemp, M.C. and Long, N.V. (1982b), 'Rybczynski's Theorem in a Context of Exhaustible Resources: The Case of Time-contingent Prices', *International Economic Review* 23(3), 699–710.

Kemp, M.C. and N.V. Long (1984a), 'Toward a More General Theory of the Order of Exploitation of Non-renewable Resource-deposits' in Kemp, M.C. and N.V. Long, eds.

Kemp, M.C. and N.V. Long (1984b), 'The Problem of Survival: An Open Economy' in Kemp, M.C. and N.V. Long, eds.

Kemp, M.C. and N.V. Long, eds. (1984c), *Essays in the Economics of Exhaustible Resources*, Elsevier Science Publishers, Amsterdam.

Kemp, M.C. and N.V. Long (1984d), 'The Role of Natural Resources in Trade Models', in Jones, R.W. and P.S. Kenen, eds., *Handbook of International Economics*, Vol. I, Elsevier Science Publishers, Amsterdam.

Kneese, A.V. (1984), 'Measuring the Benefits of Clean Air and Water', *Resources for the Future*, Washington.

Kolstad, C.D. and F.A. Wolak (1983), 'Competition in Interregional Taxation: The Case of Western Coal', *Journal of Political Economy* 91(3), 443–460.

Krautkraemer, J.A. (1987), 'The Cut-off Grade and the Theory of Extraction', *Canadian Journal of Economics* 2(1), 146–160.

Krautkraemer, J.A. (1989), 'Price Expectations, Ore Quality Selection, and the Supply of a Nonrenewable Resource', *Journal of Environmental Economics and Management* 16(3), 253–67.

Krautkraemer, J.A. (1988), 'Ore Quality Selection and the Supply Response to Nonrenewable Resource Taxation', *Mathematical and Computer Modelling* 11, 894–898.

Kremers, J.J.M. (1986), 'The Dutch Disease in the Netherlands', in Neary, J.P. and S. Van Wijnbergen, eds.

Kumar, (1988), 'On Optimal Domestic Processing of Exhaustible Natural Resource Exports', *Journal of Environmental Economics and Management* 15(3), 341–54.

La Grandville, O. de (1980), 'Capital Theory, Optimal Growth, and Efficiency Conditions with Exhaustible Resources', *Econometrica* 48(7), 1763–1776.

Lasserre, P. (1984), 'Reserves and Land Prices with Exploration Under Uncertainty', *Journal of Environmental Economics and Management* 11, 191–201.

Lasserre, P. (1985a), 'Discovery Costs as a Measure of Rent', *Canadian Journal of Economics* 18(3), 474–484.

Lasserre, P. (1985b), 'Exhaustible-Resource Extraction with Capital', in Scott A.D., ed., *Progress in Natural Resource Economics*, Oxford Economic Papers, Oxford.

116 PIERRE LASSERRE

Lasserre, P. (1989), 'Survival with a Ricardian Resource', mimeo, Université de Montréal.
Lasserre, P. and P. Ouellette (1991), 'The Measurement of Productivity and Scarcity Rents: the Case of Asbestos in Canada', *Journal of Econometrics*, forthcoming.
Lee, D.R. (1984), 'The Economics of Enforcing Pollution Taxation', *Journal of Environmental Economics and Management* **11(2)**, 147–160.
Leland, H. (1978), 'Optimal Risk Sharing and the Leasing of Natural Resources with Application to Oil and Gas on the OCS', *Quarterly Journal of Economics* **92**, 413–438.
Levhari D. and N. Liviatan (1977), 'Notes on Hotelling's Economics of Exhaustible Resources', *Canadian Journal of Economics* **10**, 177–192.
Lewis, T.R. (1979), 'The Exhaustion and Depletion of Natural Resources', *Econometrica* **47(6)**, 1569–1572.
Lewis, T.R. (1982), 'Sufficient Conditions for Extracting Least Cost Resources First', *Econometrica* **50(4)**, 1081–1083.
Lewis, T.R. and R. Schmallensee (1980), 'Oligopolistic Markets for Nonrenewable Natural Resources', *Quarterly Journal of Economics* **95**, 475–491.
Livernois, J.R. and R.S. Uhler (1987), 'Extraction Costs and the Economics of Nonrenewable Resources', *Journal of Political Economy* **95(1)**, 195–203.
Long, N.V. and H.W. Sinn (1984), 'Optimal Taxation and Economic Depreciation: A General Equilibrium Model with Capital and an Exhaustible Resource', in Kemp, M.C. and N.V. Long, eds.
Loury, G.C. (1978), 'The Optimal Exploitation of an Unknown Reserve' *Review of Economic Studies* **45**, 621–36.
Loury, G.C. (1986), 'A Theory of Oil'igoploy: Cournot Equilibrium in Exhaustible Resource Markets with Fixed Supplies', *International Economic Review* **27(2)**, 285–311.
Mackie-Mason (1987), 'Nonlinear Taxation of Risky Assets and Investment, with Application to Mining', Working Paper no 87-1, Department of Economics, University of Michigan, Ann Arbor, Michigan.
Mäler, K.-G. (1989), 'The Acid-Rain Game', mimeo, Dept. of Economics, University of Stockholm.
Malinvaud, E. (1977), *The Theory of Unemployment Reconsidered*, Oxford, Basil Blackwell.
Merrifield, J.D. (1988), 'The Impact of Selected Abatement Strategies on Transnational Pollution, the Terms of Trade, and Factor Rewards: a General Equilibrium Approach', *Journal of Environmental Economics and Management* **15(3)**, 259–284.
Miller, M.H. and C.W. Upton (1985), 'A Test of the Hotelling Valuation Principle', *Journal of Political Economy* **93(1)**, 1–25.
Mitra, T., M. Majumdar and D. Roy (1982), 'Feasible Alternatives Under Deteriorating Terms of Trade', *Journal of International Economics* **13**, 105–134.
Neary, J.P. and D.D. Purvis (1983), 'Real Adjustment and Exchange Rate Dynamics', in Frenkel, J., ed., *Exchange Rates and International Macroeconomics*, Chicago University Press, Chicago.
Neary, J.P. and S. Van Winjnbergen (1986a), *Natural Resources and the Macro-economy: a Theoretical Framework*, in Neary J.P. and S. Van Winjnbergen, eds.
Neary, J.P. and S. Van Winjnbergen, eds. (1986b), *Natural Resources and the Macroeconomy*, MIT Press, Cambridge, Massachusetts.
Newberry, D.M.G. (1981), 'Oil Price Cartels and the Problem of Dynamic Inconsistency', *Economic Journal* **21**, 617–46.
Nordhaus, W.D. (1973), 'The allocation of Energy Resources', *Brookings Papers on Economics Activity* **3**, 529–576.

Philips, L. and R.M. Harstad (1988), 'Interaction between Resource Extraction and Future Markets: A Game-theoretic Analysis', 25th Conference of the Applied Econometrics Association, Washington, D.C.

Pindyck, R.S. (1978a), 'Gains to Producers from the Cartelization of Exhaustible Resources', *Review of Economics and Statistics* **60(2)**, 238–251.

Pindyck, R.S. (1978b), 'The Optimal Exploration and Production of Nonrenewable Resources', *Journal of Political Economy* **86(5)**, 841–861.

Pindyck, R.S. (1980), 'Uncertainty and Exhaustible Resource Markets', *Journal of Political Economy* **88(6)**, 1203–1225.

Pindyck, R.S. (1982), 'Jointly Produced Exhaustible Resources', *Journal of Environmental Economics and Management* **9(4)1**, 291–303.

Pindyck, R.S. (1987), 'On Monopoly Power in Extractive Resource Markets', *Journal of Environmental Economics and Management* **14(2)**, 128–142.

Plourde, C. and D. Yeoung (1989) 'A Model of Industrial Pollution in a Stochastic Environment'. *Journal of Environmental Economics and Management* **16(2)**, 97–105.

Puu, T. (1977), 'On the Profitability of Exhausting Natural Resources', *Journal of Environmental Economics and Management* **14**, 185–199.

Quyen, N.V. (1988), 'The Optimal Depletion and Exploration of a Nonrenewable Resource', *Econometrica* **56(6)**, 1467–1471.

Quyen, N.V. (1989), 'Exhaustible Resources: A Theory of Exploration', Cahier 8905, Groupe de recherche en économie de l'énergie et des ressources naturelles, Université Laval, Québec.

Ramsey, J.B. (1980), *Bidding and Oil Leases*, JAI Press, Greenwich, Connecticut.

Raucher, M. (1987), 'Trade with Exhaustible Resource when Demand Reactions are Lagged', *European Economic Review* **31(8)**, 597–604.

Reinganum, J. and N. Stockey (1985), 'Oligopoly Extraction of a Nonrenewable Common Property Resource: The Importance of the Period of Commitment in Dynamic Games', *International Economic Review* **26(1)**, 161–73.

Ricardo, D. (1817), 'Principles of Political Economy and Taxation', in P. Sraffa and M.H. Dobbs, eds. (1951), *The Works of David Ricardo*, Cambridge University Press, Cambridge.

Robson, A.J. (1979), 'Sequential Exploitation of Uncertain Deposits of a Depletable Natural Resource', *Journal of Economic Theory* **21**, 88–110.

Salant, S. (1976), 'Exhaustible Resources and Industrial Structure: A Nash-Cournot Approach to the World Oil Market', *Journal of Political Economy* **84(5)**, 1079–1093.

Salant, S. (1979), 'Staving off the Backstop: Dynamic Limit-Pricing with a Kinked Demand Curve', in *Advances in the Economics of Energy and Resources*, Vol. 2, 187–204, JAI Press, Inc.

Salant, S. (1983), 'The Vulnerability of Price Stabilization Schemes to Speculative Attack', *Journal of Political Economy* **91(1)**, 1–38.

Salant, S., M. Eswaran, and T. Lewis (1983), 'The Length of Optimal Extraction Programs When Depletion Affects Extraction Costs', *Journal of Economic Theory* **31(2)**, 264–74.

Salant, S. and D.W. Henderson (1978), 'Market Anticipations of Government Policies and the Price of Gold' *Journal of Political Economy* **86(4)**, 627–48.

Schultze, W.D. (1974), 'The Optimal Use of Nonrenewable Resources: The Theory of Extraction', *Journal of Environmental Economics and Management* **1(1)**, 53–73.

Scott, A.D. (1976), 'Who Should Get Natural Resource Revenues', in Scott, A.D., ed., *Natural Resource Economics: A Test of Federalism*, University of British Columbia Press, Vancouver.

Simons, P. (1977), 'Optimum Taxation and Natural Resources', *Recherches Economiques de Louvain* **43(2)**.

Slade, M.E. (1982a), 'Cycles in Natural Resource Commodity Prices: An Analysis of the Frequency Domain', *Journal of Environmental Economics and Management* **9**, 138–148.

Slade, M.E. (1982b), 'Cycles in Natural-resource Commodity Prices: An Analysis of the Time Domain', *Journal of Environmental Economics Management* **9(2)**, 122–137.

Slade, M.E. (1984), 'Tax Policy and the Supply of Exhaustible Resources: Theory and Practice', *Land Economics* **60(2)**, 133–147.

Slade, M.E. (1988), 'Grade Selection under Uncertainty: Least Cost Last and Other Anomalies', *Journal of Environmental Economics and Management* **15(2)**, 189–205.

Smith, V.K. (1979), 'Natural Resource Scarcity: A Statistical Analysis', *Review of Economics and Statistics* **61(3)**, 423–427.

Smith, V.K. (1979), *Scarcity and Growth Reconsidered*, Johns Hopkins University Press (for *Resources for the Future*), Baltimore.

Solow, R.M. (1974a), 'The Economics of Resources and the Resources of Economics', *American Economic Review*, Papers and Proceedings.

Solow, R.M. (1974b), 'Intergenerational Equity and Exhaustible Resources', *Review of Economic Studies*, Symposium.

Solow, R.M. (1977), 'Monopoly, Uncertainty, and Exploration' in A. Blinder and P. Friedman, eds., *Natural Resources, Uncertainty, and General Equilibrium Systems*, New York.

Solow, R.M. and F.Y. Wan (1977), 'Extraction Costs in the Theory of Exhaustible Resources', *Bell Journal of Economics* **7(2)**, 359–370.

Stiglitz, J.E. (1974a), 'Growth with Exhaustible Natural Resources: The Competitive Economy', *Review of Economic Studies*, Symposium, 123–138.

Stiglitz, J.E. (1974b), 'Growth with Exhaustible Resources: Efficient and Optimal Growth Paths', *Review of Economic Studies*, Symposium, 139–152.

Stiglitz, J.E. (1976), 'Monopoly and the Rate of Extraction of Exhaustible Resources', *American Economic Review* **66(4)**, 655–661.

Stiglitz, J.E. and P. Dasgupta (1982), 'Market Structure and Resource Depletion: A Contribution to the Theory of Intertemporal Monopolistic Competition', *Journal of Economic Theory* **28(1)**, 128–164.

Stollery, K.R. (1983), 'Mineral Depletion with Cost as the Extraction Limit: A Model Applied to the Behavior of Prices in the Nickel Industry', *Journal of Environmental Economics and Management* **10(2)**, 151–165.

Swierzbinski, J.E. and R. Mendelsohn (1989) 'Information and Exhaustible Resources: A Bayesian Analysis' *Journal of Environmental Economics Management* **16(3)**, 193–208.

The Economist (1977), 'The Dutch Disease', nov. 26-dec. 2, 82–83.

The Economist (1988), 'Asia's Migrant Workers', sept. 10-16, 21–24.

Tietenberg, T.H. (1985), 'Emissions Trading: An Exercise in Reforming Pollution Policy', *Resources for the Future*, Washington.

Ulph, A.M. (1982), 'Modelling Partially Cartelized Markets for Exhaustible Resources', in Eichhorn, H., R. Henn, U. Newmann and R.W. Shephard, eds., *Economic Theory of Natural Resources*, Physica-Verlag, Würburg-Wien, 269–291.

Ulph A.M. and G.M. Folie (1980), 'Exhaustible Resources and Cartels: an Intertemporal Nash-Cournot Model', *Canadian Journal of Economics* **13(4)**, 645–658.

Virmani, A. (1986), 'Efficiency of Practical Resource Rent Tax System: Threshold Rates and Income Taxes', Report no DRD164, World Bank, Washington, D.C.
Warr, P.G. (1986), 'Indonesia's Other Dutch Disease: Economic Effects of the Petroleum Boom', in Neary, J.P. and S. Van Wijnbergen, eds.
Wijnbergen, S.V. (1984), 'The Dutch Disease: A Disease After All?', *The Economic Journal* **24**, 41–55.
Withagen, C. (1985), *Economic Theory and International Trade in Natural Exhaustible Resources*, Springer-Verlag, Berlin.

Index

Acid rain 56
Aggregation 11
Anti-Heckscher–Ohlin 59
Arbitrage 40

Backstop 15
Bayesian up-dating 13
Bonus bid 108
Booming sector 70

Capacity 15
Capital 14, 23
Capital accumulation 58
Capital, book value 100
Capital, taxation 99
Capital-asset-pricing 41
Cartel 31, 34
Classical unemployment 74
Cleanup 44, 49, 52
Closed loop 31, 35
Commitment 30, 37
Competition 16
Competitive equilibrium 16, 53
Composite ore 44, 47
Computable international general
  equilibrium 80
Conservationists 28
Consistency 35
Consumption 23
Corporate income tax 82, 99
Corporate income tax, non-extractive
  sectors 104
Cournot–Nash 30
Cumulated extraction 22

Damage 52
Debt rescheduling 80
Degradation 24
Deindustrialization 73
Depletion allowance 99, 103, 109
Developed countries 77
Developing countries, capital surplus 77

Developing countries, poor 77
Discoveries 12, 106
Distortive effects 83
Diversification, cone of 62
Domestic processing 81
Dumping sites 49, 52
Duopoly 30, 31
Duration 86
Dutch Disease 69
Dutch Disease, policy implications 76
Dutch Disease, theoretical
  framework 70
Dynamic consistency 31, 35
Dynamic inconsistency 35, 37

Economic reserves 10
Effective tax rate 99, 103
Elasticity, demand 29, 90
Elasticity, of substitution 23, 34
Empirical tests 37
Endowments 59
Energy 22, 50
Exchange rate 69
Exhaustion 7, 10
Expectations 17, 35
Exploration 12, 30, 104
Exploration, corporate income tax 107
Exploration, stochastic treatment 107
Export tariff 82
Extensive margin 105
Externality 44, 48, 77
Extraction costs 9
Extraction period 91, 96, 97

Factor endowment 12, 60, 65
Factor intensity 60
Factor movement effect 71
Factor price equalization 64, 67
Factor rigidities 76
Franchise tax 84, 86
Fringe 31
Full marginal cost 10

120

Full-employment equilibrium 74
Futures markets 18, 80

Government intervention 48
Grade selection 40
Greenhouse 49
Growth 22

Heckscher–Ohlin 64, 67, 25
Heckscher–Ohlin model 59, 73
Heckscher–Ohlin, generalized model 59, 65
Heckscher–Ohlin, hybrid model 60
Heterogeneity 9
Homogeneous 47
Hotelling 4
Hotelling endowments 65
Hotelling margin 24
Hotelling principle 38
Hotelling rent 6
Hotelling rule 5, 7, 38, 47, 63
Hotelling rule, modified 51
Hotelling Valuation principle 42

Import tariff 82
Imported resource 56
Infant industry 77
Inflation 69
Instruments 82
Intensive margin 105

Joint production 43, 44

Keynesian unemployment 74

Lagged expectations 43
Leases 82
Lerner index 28
License fee 84

Macroeconomy 69
Market power 27, 81
Market price 45
Martingale 40
Monopoly 27, 81
Multiple deposits 14

Nash 30, 31
Neutrality 102, 107, 108, 109
Non-appropriable 49
Non-cooperative 56

Oligopoly 15, 30
One-sector growth model 57
Open economy 58
Open loop 35
Optimal extraction path 85
Optimal taxation 108, 109
Order-of-extraction 15

Physical depreciation 100
Policy instruments 55
Pollution 43, 49
Pollution abatement 50, 55
Pollution, cumulative 50
Pollution, general equilibrium 54
Pollution, transnational 54
Population growth 27
Price studies 37
Price trajectories 38, 58
Product taxes 55
Productivity 39, 55
Profit tax 84
Property rights 21
Property tax 88, 96
Property tax, *ad valorem* 84
Property tax, fixed 84
Public intervention 53
Pure profit tax 89
Pure rent tax 107

Rate of return tax 82, 84
Rate of return tax, progressive 99
Rational expectations 35
Recycling oil revenues 80
Regulations 53
Rent 39, 47, 86
Repressed inflation 74
Reserves, ultimate 95
Residual demand 32
Residual value 83
Resource bonanza 69
Resource endowment 22
Resource intensities 65
Resource price 40, 46
Resource rent tax 84
Resource rents 39, 78
Resource scarcity 38
Resource essential 25
Resource, necessary 23
Resource, useful 22
Ricardian 10
Ricardian factors 59
Ricardian margin 24

Ricardian rents 6
Ricardo 4, 8
Risk neutrality 109
Royalty 82, 84, 87
Royalty, *ad valorem* 84, 88
Rybczynski 64, 67, 73

Scarcity 10
Scarcity rent 5, 6, 39
Severance tax 20, 82, 87, 95
Severance tax, *ad valorem* 84, 88
Shadow price 41
Simultaneous exploitation 15
Social optimum 48, 51
Social optimum, taxation 83
Specialization 60, 69
Specialization, capital intensive
    industry 69
Specialization, resource intensive
    industry 69
Speculative attacks 21
Speculative purchases 31
Spending effect 71
Stability 16
Stackelberg 30, 35
Start-up date, endogenous 105
Steady-state 17
Stolper-Samuelson 64, 67
Storage 48
Strategic behaviour 110
Sub-game perfectness 31, 35
Substitutes 15
Substitution elasticities 33
Substitution, capital 57

Survival 22, 27, 56
Survival, trade 57

Tax depreciation 100
Tax function 84
Tax incidence 110
Tax instruments 108
Tax on capital 24
Taxation 53, 55, 82
Taxation, Cournot-Nash
    competition 110, 111
Taxation, Hotelling world 83
Taxation, Ricardian world 90
Taxation, Stackelberg behaviour 110
Taxation, strategic behaviour 110
Technological change 27, 58
Terminal date 85
Terms of trade 57, 60
Time autonomous tax function 93
Time consistency 41
Trade 56, 59
Trade equilibrium 59, 63
Trade theorems 59, 64
Trade, Hotelling resources 59
Transfer price 45, 49
Transportation costs 81
Two-sector economy 57

Ultimate extraction 96
Unemployment 69, 74

Waste 50, 52
Welfare 16

T - #0091 - 230425 - C0 - 216/138/8 - PB - 9780415849333 - Gloss Lamination